WITHDRAWN

Intellectuals at the Crossroads

INTELLECTUALS AT THE CROSSROADS
The Indian Situation

Akhileshwar Jha

VIKAS PUBLISHING HOUSE PVT LTD
New Delhi Bombay Bangalore Calcutta Kanpur

VIKAS PUBLISHING HOUSE PVT LTD
5 Ansari Road, New Delhi 110002
Savoy Chambers, 5 Wallace Street, Bombay 400001
10 First Main Road, Gandhi Nagar, Bangalore 560009
8/1-B Chowringhee Lane, Calcutta 700016
80 Canning Road, Kanpur 208004

Copyright © Akhileshwar Jha, 1977

ISBN 0 7069 0529 6

1V02J1801

Rs 36

Printed at Roopabh Printers, Vishwas Nagar, Shahdara, Delhi-110032

PREFACE

The intellectual anywhere in the world is a typical product of the maturity of our modern age which was ushered in by the renaissance in Europe of the sixteenth century. He is characterized by deep faith in the immense possibilities of modern science and technology, as a means to gain more and more knowledge of nature's endless mysteries and to exploit its inexhaustible resources in the service of man. In his philosophical outlook, he is a rationalist-humanist. To him, man is wholly a social being; that is, man can realize his own potentialities, his own self, only by living in society and never by cutting himself off from it. But the intellectual would firmly reject any suggestion to the effect that man exists for society. He would rather put it the other way round: society exists for man. The intellectual believes that various social institutions exist primarily to free man from his bondage to ignorance and blind faith, to lend support to his eternally inquiring spirit, and to induce him to give creative expression to his individuality. All this, in return, enriches the social institutions too.

In India the intellectual was born during the hey-day of the British rule which introduced modernity into society. Later it was the intellectual who roused the people to fight for political freedom. And finally, after independence, it was he who acquired the responsibility of ruling the country.

This book attempts to examine the nature of the rise of the Indian intellectual and his triumph against his social and cultural background. It is not addressed to scholars and specialists. It is primarily meant for such general intellectual readers as are concerned with the crisis deepening at the heart of contemporary Indian society.

Chapter Eleven of the book entitled, *An Elite Without Identity*, has already appeared in a slightly modified form in *The Sunday Statesman* (New Delhi, 2 May 1977).

AKHILESHWAR JHA

CONTENTS

PART 1
THE BACKGROUND

CHAPTER ONE	The Making of the Intellectual Community	3
CHAPTER TWO	Modernity and the Intellectual	11
CHAPTER THREE	The Western and the Indian Intellectuals	19
CHAPTER FOUR	In Search of an Indian Tradition	26
CHAPTER FIVE	The Question of Identity	34
CHAPTER SIX	The Promise of the Freedom Struggle	42

PART 2
THE SITUATION TODAY

CHAPTER SEVEN	Post-Independence Dissipation	55
CHAPTER EIGHT	Round and Round the Prickly-Pear	64
CHAPTER NINE	The Language Tangle	73
CHAPTER TEN	Educational and Cultural Doldrums	83
CHAPTER ELEVEN	An Elite Without Identity: Delhi Intellectuals X-Rayed	94
CHAPTER TWELVE	Responsibilities of the Indian Intellectual	103
	Select Bibliography	111

PART 1

THE BACKGROUND

Chapter One

THE MAKING OF THE INTELLECTUAL COMMUNITY

Inbuilt into every society today there is a small and disorganized community of intellectuals. It has formed slowly all by itself in course of the growth and development of highly complex modern knowledge. Its membership is open to every one who has adequate qualifications, but there is no office to receive applications for admission and no one to process them for consideration. One gains entrance to this community by merit of his work alone, and this merit is proved by the nature of the contribution which the work makes to the existing body of knowledge.

In a wider sense, the community is composed of all those who are educated, not merely literate, and are doing jobs which require the exercise more of mental then of manual power. From this point of view not only scientists, philosophers, social thinkers, educationists, lawyers and literary writers, but also bureaucrats, business executives and even office clerks can claim to be legitimate members of this community. So they are, no doubt. Yet they are the secondary members of the community, and constitute a vast majority within the community.

The nucleus of it, however, is composed of a tiny group of people who are assiduously preoccupied with the production of knowledge. These few individuals are the primary intellectuals. Although they have a tendency to collect in metropolitan cities, some of them might stay and work elsewhere. They never work in groups, even when they may live in one city. They remain familiar with the works of each other, and take these meticulously into consideration in their constant endeavour of extending the frontiers of modern knowledge.

Thus the primary intellectuals are the producers of knowledge while the secondary intellectuals are the distributors as well as the consumers of knowledge. The merely literate too, sometimes even the illiterate, could be among the consumers.

This pattern exists more or less independently in every society. At the same time there exists a larger intellectual community encompassing all societies, the members of which are dispersed all over the world. This world intellectual community commands the highest authority today. It has, of course, no means to exercise its authority. It has in fact no need to, though an appeal of this authority cuts across national and social boundaries and plays a vital role in the progress of society in any part of the world.

People are never coerced to obey this authority. They pay obeisance to it voluntarily, and much more whole-heartedly than to any other authority. They pay obeisance not to the authority of the man as such but to the knowledge he has created, and they absorb the knowledge into their own thinking.

The membership of this world intellectual community is not confined to people from one or two nations. Intellectuals from any nation can join the community, if their qualifications measure up to the world standards of achievement.

As every secondary intellectual may have potentialites for becoming a primary intellectual, so every primary intellectual of a particular society may have potentialities for becoming a member of the world intellectual community. There is no bar anywhere. No rules are in force. It is an absolutely free community. Any restraint imposed upon it from any quarter tends to breed forces of decay and disintegration.

The community of intellectuals as it exists today began to be formed with the advent of the Renaissance in Europe, which was the first intellectual movement—a pioneering one which was followed by a series of epoch-making intellectual movements in succeeding centuries. The Reformation, the Industrial Revolution, the French Revolution, the American War of Independence, the Communist Revolutions, etc. have all been created and conducted by intellectuals. In the present century, the freedom struggle in Asian and African countries have been, by and large, the handiwork of intellectuals. From among them come the thinkers and leaders who initiate and guide the process of radical changes in society.

Not that in the past there were no intellectuals. They belong to the history of any ancient civilization. In fact, at any time the civilization has been their creation, but intellectuals of ancient times had to contend with severe limitations. The first ever intellectuals were the earliest scribes who came into being with the introduction of writing in the Middle East, about 2000 B.C. In India, the date of the introduction of the alphabet and of digits would be even earlier. Before that, knowledge was passed on orally from generation to generation. In India the oral tradition of teaching—that is of imparting and receiving knowledge—was in vogue in Sanskrit schools until recently. Even today the teachers in Sanskrit *pathshalas* insist on more oral and less written work.

The earliest intellectuals, the scribes, were born in their nascent form only with the introduction of writing, of alphabet and digits. The mysteries of knowledge were now embodied in enigmatic signs and dots which could be deciphered only by the scribes. Thus gradually emerged a group of people, with a special knowledge of script and figures, who were indispensable for trade and business, as also for administration. The scribes came to acquire a special status in the society, as an inalienable ally of the trade and ruling class—a characteristic which modern intellectuals seem to share with them.

Later on, with time and the crumbling of the ancient structure of the society, the role of the scribes became diversified. Keeping accounts and recording the orders of the ruling chief was no longer the only work to be done. Some of the scribes turned to recording what they saw, and had learnt orally about the deeds of the deities and heroes. Therein lay the origin of literary writing and the birth of a new class of writers.

At the time writers of this sort were only one small group of intellectuals. Other kinds of intellectuals arose in the form of magicians, soothsayers and so on, the earliest prototypes of the modern scientists, to command greater respect and obedience from the people. Often they turned into rulers, and then engaged the scribes to keep record of things and offer advice on matters relating to obedience to authority and war. Sometimes the scribes wrote some pieces of adulation to please their masters, in the hope of getting rewards.

With the advent of Christianity in Europe, the Christian saints and fathers came to perform the intellectual role for their societies. They were aligned with the rulers of kingdoms. The latter, in fact, depended for their existence on the former. In ancient India too, the Brahmin priests were the intellectuals of the time, and enjoyed the same privileges in the courts.

Thus before the coming of the Renaissance in Europe, intellectuals, of whatever sort they were, existed as close allies and supporters of the rulers. After the Renaissance, or rather with it, a severance began to occur between intellectuals on the one hand and rulers on the other.

This was bound to happen. Knowledge, for the first time in human history, began to be based on empirical evidence and was severed from mere speculation. No longer could knowledge be distorted to serve the ends of this clique or that, this king or that. It was acquiring its own independent entity. Again, for the first time, knowledge was freed from mystery and magic and became decipherable in terms of clear logical and mathematical proof. Knowledge came to be open to all who cared to acquire it. It affected even those who merely heard about the new knowledge, and found the ocular proof of it around themselves, or merely felt it on their pulse.

Since this knowledge emerged from independent intellectual pursuits of people with indomitable spirits such as Kepler and Galileo, and since it conflicted with the immediate interests of the authorities, a fierce tussle ensued between the intellectuals and the authorities. Often it led to the worst kind of oppression of the intellectuals by the authorities, who did not at times hesitate to put their enemy to death.

What, however, helped the intellectuals eventually win the struggle decisively was the introduction of the printing press by Caxton. It frustrated the attempt of rulers to exterminate the intellectuals whose knowledge weakened their authority. The fruits of intellectual activities now came not merely to be written by one man in one copy, but thousands of copies of a book could be prepared and distributed in relatively little time. The kings could kill the intellectuals but their work remained intact to make impact on the people, to inspire them to bear the torch of knowledge and take it further.

Detached from kings and their hirelings, the intellectuals came to find their new ally in the masses. Not that all of them happened to read the books written and printed. But a few more intelligent and ambitious of them certainly read them, and explained the message to others who followed the few. In times of need, intellectuals could fan up the passions of the masses with the immediate appeal of the new knowledge, and with carefully phrased rhetoric to bring about a state of revolution.

This pattern of antagonistic relationship, between the intellectual and the established authority, continues more or less to exist in all societies even today. This does not mean, however, that either during or after the Renaissance all intellectuals were opposed to the rulers. Actually, a large number of them, a very large number, were not. They still served their masters happily and with absolutely no reservations. Today too, the same picture is to be seen all over the world. With the spread of mass education, and the emergence of democracy and communism as the two dominant forms of government, more and more intellectuals are inducted into the establishment, or try to join it on their own.

Nevertheless, in every society the struggle between the intellectual and the establishment exists eternally in some form or the other. Even in communist Russia, where the conflict was proclaimed to have come to an end with the intellectuals themselves coming into power and running the whole state machinery, the tussle has arisen from time to time between the intellectuals in power and those out of it. In the liberal west European and American societies, however, the tussle breeds creative results. It generates the forces of social progress to higher and still higher levels. It thus prevents stratification and stagnation of creative energy inherent in the members of society itself.

In this struggle between intellectuals and the established authority, not all educated people in any society participate. Education alone does not make an intellectual, though of course, education—particularly in the real sense of the term—is the basic constituent of an intellectual. It may be formal education with diplomas and degrees, or it may be informal, self-taught education. More essentially the latter, for the former kind of education is generally of the utilitarian kind. It is primarily a means to finding employment.

Not that intellectuals do not seek employment, or can do without getting jobs for their livelihood, unless they are exceptionally rich like Tagore and Tolstoy. More often than not, great intellectuals have emerged from such professions as trade and commerce, and even from the class of manual labourers.

An intellectual, in the sense in which he is understood today, is made of a particular temper and a certain bent of mind. For earning his bread he may do any work, but his mind is preoccupied not so much with immediate and particular things, but with the shape of things to come in general terms, and with the contribution he can make in determining this shape. The future is his domain of contemplation, but the future always related to the present, never detached from it. His contemplation is rationally organized taking into account the various known facts and figures in his discipline. But mere contemplation is not enough. An intellectual must have cultivated the art of expressing himself in his language most effectively, or even through other media such as colour and sound, using symbols and metaphors embodying his ideas and experiences. His concern is society, or rather, society in relation to its members, and how to shape it with a view to creating conditions for the fuller realisation of the potentialities with which men and women are born.

In today's world the producers of ideas have happened to grow and collect at only a few of the world's big metropolises situated in western Europe and America. Ideas produced at those centres are consumed not only in the countries of their origin, but in almost all countries of the world, excluding the communist countries, sometimes not even excluding them.

In a broad sense, these producers of ideas at the metropolises and the consumers of these ideas in various countries of the world, which become the provinces, constitute the world body of intellectuals. The metropolises are the centres of intellectual authority which is obeyed readily and even happily in the provinces. The ideas have a deep and invigorating appeal, and the people respond to them sometimes warily, sometimes enthusiastically, and sometimes even antagonistically, depending upon their cultural background, their current political situation and their level of economic progress.

Within this world community of intellectuals exist smaller communities in different countries, under different social systems. The centre of this national intellectual community is constituted by the leading social, political and economic thinkers, scientists, jurists, journalists and writers, and provides fresh, original ideas relevant both immediately and in the long run. These leading intellectuals may not be leading figures in bureaucracy, or semi-government organizations. In fact, it is essential that they be independent of obligations to the establishment; for only then can they develop a truly rational and objective approach to the problems confronting the society.

Nor it is necessary that the ideas of intellectuals be put to the test of immediate application, to verify their soundness or phoneyness. For these ideas generally do not apply to particular problems. They are related to the broader and more fundamental issues of man's relation to society, and of organizing social institutions in such a way as to release his creative potentialities.

Some leading intellectuals of a national intellectual community may become members of the world intellectual body, by means of the validity of their ideas not merely to national but international problems, and by virtue of their deep concern for fundamental human problems which are the same all over the world. When this happens, another centre springs up in the world intellectual community, a centre which only a few years ago was a province. In certain respects London, the unchallenged centre till about the second world war, has become the province of Paris and New York.

In India, soon after Independence, a possibility of Calcutta, Delhi, Bombay, Madras becoming centres of great intellectual activity seemed to be in evidence. After a decade and a half it began to be clear that this possibility was something of an illusion. Consequently, India remains a province of the U.K. and the U.S.A., in almost all areas of intellectual activity.

Why should it be so ? In fact, the situation appears to be paradoxical. In the last decade of the nineteenth century and the first three decades of the twentieth century, when India was under British rule, it produced an array of intellectuals such as Tagore, Gandhi, Tilak, Jawaharlal Nehru, Radhakrishnan and others. Each one of them potentially was capable of claiming membership to the world intellectual body, on the basis of having generated cogent and solid traditions of thought in their own society. After Independence, whatever traditions of thought and action had been generated begin to disintegrate and decay, and soon get lost in the babel of utter confusion. The explanation generally given, that intellectual thinking has declined on a world-wide basis in the present century, particularly after the last war, is not really satisfying. The world is still producing intellectuals, though in fewer numbers than those of the preceding century, but with more relevance to the world we live in today. The Indian intellectuals have no stand in their contribution to the development of world thought.

Is this due to economic backwardness and the political immaturity of the Indian people? It could be. Apparently there appears to be some connection between economic affluence and intellectual efflorescence. If it was Britain, with its empire encompassing a large part of the globe as the intellectual leader in the nineteenth century, so it is America today with its economic affluence. Yet it is not always so. France under German occupation had a spurt of intellectuals who provided effective leadership to the resistance movement. Russia produced Tolstoy and Dostoevsky when materially it was much poorer than it is today. Finally, there is the case of India itself. Economically, it is better off than it was under the British Raj. Intellectually, it remains backward.

The reasons are certainly deeper and need to be explored in a wider context.

Chapter Two

MODERNITY AND THE INTELLECTUAL

The formation of the intellectual community begins in any society with the process of modernization. The two processes accompany each other so closely as though to appear to be one. In fact, if the history of society is any evidence, they are one and the same. No society has been modernized without the vigorous participation of its intellectuals. And again, to put it in another way which, in effect, is the same, no intellectual community can come into being in a society which is not modernized.

The European Renaissance, for example, was as much the creation of the intellectual as the intellectual was the creation of the Renaissance. That is, the new intellectual became an independent and strong social force to reckon with, and played for the first time in history a decisive role in the shaping of the social and political institutions. He not merely provided ideas but commanded a force to pressurize the political and administrative authorities, to implement them, even if only partially at a time.

The process which began with the European Renaissance continued to develop through the successive centuries, encompassing a larger part of the globe with diversification in different societies. As the pace of modernization picked up speed in Europe, with the progress of science and technology in the early years of the eighteenth century, the intellectuals came to acquire a more and more dominant role in the social set-up, more particularly in Britain. Among European nations, Britain is perhaps the only exception to the rule of social progress through violent revolution. This was possible because of the nation's intellectuals who were alert, responsible, and responsive to the needs of the society, who absorbed the revolutionary forces latent in the process of social development and put them into the form of a well-charted program of orderly action. If Britain did not have to undergo a bloody revolution like the French Revolution, it was because, in a large part, of its intellectuals. They determined the course of Britain's relatively smooth and easy change from feudalistic to industrial society—a change which was potentially fraught with so much violence.

The fruits of scientific discoveries and technological inventions remained largely limited to Europe for almost a whole century. All of Europe was one culture, and had inherited the same intellectual tradition from the earliest times. For almost a whole millennium Christianity had reigned supreme in the continent. It is no longer a paradox to say that Christianity itself prepared the European mind for the Renaissance, that is, for the advent of the modern empirical age. This it had done primarily in two ways. One, it permitted interpretation and reinterpretation of its tenets, which encouraged, or at least did not kill, the spirit of inquiry. At first, it was an inquiry into the meanings of Christian messages and Christian rituals with a view to justifying them. This developed into an inquiry into the nature of the things around created by God, with a view to praise His work.

This spirit of inquiry led to far-reaching scientific discoveries, though the early discoverers themselves were inspired more by religious faith than otherwise. Kepler and Galileo, and even the great Newton, were all men of faith. By discovering the the laws which governed nature they wanted to show the wonderful grand design of God's creation. Their discoveries in effect gave the first severe jolt to the establishment, but their work had been done in the spirit of religious faith. If Newton escaped the fate of Kepler and Galileo, it was because by Newton's time the intellectual climate in England had changed a great deal. Free inquiry into the nature of things, religious or secular, had become possible, even in a sense, respectable.

Another way in which Christianity prepared the way for the emergence of the modern mind was its contribution to the revival of the ancient Greek learning and literature, in the fourteenth and fifteenth centuries. In its earliest stages of development, Christianity had adopted quite a few rituals, Greek and Roman, giving them Christian colour by substituting new names and modifying the manner of performance. Thus Christianity had not killed barbaric culture, but had absorbed it completely into its own. Thereby it had made the ancient Greek and Roman cultures an important ingredient of the all-European Christian culture.

When revival of learning took place in Italy, France, Germany and England in the fourteenth-fifteenth century, it naturally originated from inquiry into some of those aspects of the Christian culture which had been assimilated from the Greek and Roman culture. Soon, however, the revival of classical learning led to the creation of attitudes and values opposed to the ones belonging to the established Christian mores.

Thus, in an essential sense, modernity is a child of Christian culture itself. In any case, they have lived and grown in harmony with each other. This has largely been possible because of the perseverance of the intellectuals to constantly reinterpret Christianity, with a view to adapting it to modernity.

In Africa and Asia it has been a different story altogether. By and large, they remained completely devoid of the advantages of the modern scientific discoveries and technological inventions for a very long time, for none of them had taken place outside Europe. Even if centres of discoveries and inventions had been next door to nations in Africa and Asia, it is far from certain that the people of these continents would have taken to new knowledge easily and quickly. What would have prevented them—and prevents them actually even today —is their own culture, particularly in Asia, which leaves no room for any spirit of free inquiry. Left to themselves, it is doubtful if they would have become even half as modernized as they are today. They took to modernization under the impact of the long colonial rule. Therefore, not suprisingly, their intellectuals are mostly Westernized and seem uprooted from their own soil.

India fortunately happened to come under the British rule. The French or the Dutch rule, with different turns of historical events, could also have been possible. If India, along with other Afro-Asian nations, was fated to become a colony of a modernized European power, it was fortunate in becoming eventually Britain's colony. It was so not only because Britain was merely the strongest of the powers contending for colonizing India in the eighteenth century. Britain at that time happened to be the most civilized, cultured and intellectually alive country in Europe. India came into close contact with the British intellectuals, which eventually bred a native band of intellectuals, who in turn initiated the demand for modernization. An awareness of the need for political freedom itself was born later, in consequence of the process of modernizing the Indian society. Had the process of modernization, however inadequate, not been initiated by British rule, there would have emerged no modern intellectuals. Consequently, in all probability, there would have been no demand for political freedom.

It would be wrong to suggest that the Britishers deliberately created the intellectuals with the primary intention of benefiting India. What they did was to introduce in the country the kind and extent of modernization which would help them consolidate their empire, and make administration easy in such a vast country. This was actually their basic objective in bringing English education to India, and constructing a vast network of communication and transport—the two things which laid the firm foundation of the modernization of Indian society, and initiated other significant changes, both external (environmental) and internal (psychological). They were revolutionary changes with far-reaching consequences, and such changes as these had never occurred before in the history of the country.

The Britishers never attempted to sow the seeds of modernization here, nor those of intellectualization. England was the home of both of these, and a few privileged Indians were allowed to go there to become modern and intellectual, and presumably to turn into supporters of the Raj. For quite a long time this was the case; but after the increased pace of modernization, and with a larger number of intellectuals having imbibed modern liberal ideas, the demand for political freedom began to be voiced by a number of outstanding British trained intellectuals.

The point to note here is that India had no intellectuals in the sense in which they are known today, before the establishment of the Britsh Raj. This introduced certain essential aspects of modernization, namely, liberal, rationalistic, science-based education, as well as modern means of communication and transport. These two things brought the farflung parts of India closer, tended to instil into its people a sense of belonging to this vast land, and induced them to think of life's problems in an entirely different way from the people of the previous generation.

It cannot be denied that India, long before the British Raj, had produced great minds. Before the light of Christian civilization dawned on Europe, even before its ancient Greek and Roman civilizations, India had great poets and philosophical thinkers. They were the unknown authors of the *Vedas*, the *Upanishads* and the *Puranas*—not to mention some of the well known names of the later periods, such as Panini, Manu, Charvak, Chanakya and Shankaracharya.

These great minds were inhibited by the limitation of their age, so that we cannot regard them as intellectuals. Their greatness was of the kind of isolated individual excellences. Individually they reached high points of speculative thought and imaginative ideas, which did not get embodied in social institutions. In other words, their thought and ideas, otherwise marvels of abstruse philosophic reasoning, were not integrated with the fabric of day-to-day living in society. They did not primarily feel responsible for the task of social construction. In fact, they could not have done so in those times, for the formation of society itself was still in a rather fluid state.

Victories and defeats in numerous battles, fought between clans, formed or destroyed societies. The laws were laid down in accordance with the wishes of the victorious chiefs and kings, and were to remain in force only till they were not in turn defeated by other chiefs and kings. The thinkers and poets of those days naturally clung to the victorious chiefs and kings, and did not feel concerned about the real living conditions of the common folk. This is evident from the nature of ancient India's literary philosophical works. While we are amazed with their philosophic queries, we know next to nothing about the actual and everyday living conditions of the time.

No mind, however intelligent and powerful, can be legitimately regarded as intellectual unless he is socially responsible, unless his intellectual work has a bearing on the life of his society From this deep social concern springs the rationality of the true intellectual, in his attitude towards life. No stable society can be built without the intellectuals. Nor can intellectuals have a sense of fulfillment apart from society.

Another characteristic which distinguishes an intelligent from a mere intelligent mind is this : he regards his work as a link in the unending process of social development, towards an almost utopian state when it will afford fullest opportunities to its members to realise their own potentialities. An intellectual believes in the perpetual social progress, which the ancient Indian thinkers were not in a position to do. For one thing, they could not have had a historical sense which is indispensable for acquiring a belief in social progress, because history itself—particularly the history of human civiliziation—began with them.

Therefore, to say that the ancient Indian great minds were not intellectual is not to denigrate their achievements. It is merely to stress that the intellectual is a typical product of modern society based on complex technology, heavy industrialization, urbanization, and of a political system which guarantees full individual freedom. Almost as a rule, the more modern a society, the more scope it creates for fruitful intellectual activities.

Now the Indian society began to be modernized under British rule, and with that emerged the Indian intellectual. The imposed and limited modernization produced only halfhearted intellectuals in general, with negligible exceptions. Had the urge for modernization come from within the society, or even after imposition, had it had taken to modernization wholeheartedly, the role of the Indian intellectual would have been more meaningful and the course of history perhaps different.

Modernity is almost a pre-condition, or an accompanying condition, for the rise of the intellectual. This becomes clear when we find that the attributes which make a man modern are basically the same which are those of the intellectual. Every typically modern man is potentially an intellectual.

Alex Inkeles in an essay on "The Modernization of Man"[1] mentions certain salient characteristics of a modern man which distinguish him from the traditionalist in any society. They are, according to him, of two kinds, external and internal. Of the former the typical characteristics are well known: "urbanization, education, mass communication, industrialization, politicization." A typically modern man is one who has acquired modern university education, lives in an urban centre, works in an industry or a factory, or a scientifically organized firm, or a public or private office, reads the newspapers, and responds to public events in the light of his own reason and capacity for understanding.

Inkeles stresses that the mere presence of the external setting does not necessarily make a man living in it modern. It is only, says Inkeles, "when he has undergone a change of spirit—has acquired certain new ways of thinking, feeling and acting—that we come to consider him truly modern."[2] There are certain attributes of this change of spirit. A modern man is always ready for new experience. Second, he is concerned with problems not merely arising out of his immediate environment, but also he develops an ability to form his own opinion about them. Third, he is a believer in democratic values. He is aware of the diversity of approaches to a problem and multiplicity of views about things. Fourth, he is concerned more with the present than with the past, and is forward-looking. Fifth, he is very much time conscious: he has fixed hours of work, believes in the value of punctuality, and manages his affairs in an orderly manner. Sixth, he believes in dominating the environment in order to advance his purpose, rather than being dominated by it. Seventh, he believes that the world is calculable, that it could be improved through social institutions under human control. Eighth, he is a believer in science and technology. Lastly, he believes in the equality of men before law, and in distributive justice.

These attributes which characterize a modern man are basic to the intellectual. But while no one can develop into an intellectual without first becoming truly modern, not all modern

[1] Myron Weiner, ed., *Modernization*, Basic Books, New York, 1966.
[2] *Ibid.*, p. 140.

men or women can be intellectuals in the true sense of the term. In the intellectual the characteristics of a modern man become a great deal more accentuated. He looks much farther ahead into the future and, at the same time, deeper into the problems confronting man in society. He is a man of well organized ideas, with a corresponding program of action to implement them through social and political institutions. He is, indeed, a creator of ideas, created out of digesting his systematic observations of society, his mastery over the existing knowledge in his field and his own personal experience. Over and above merely being modern, the intellectual is a man of thought, ideas, and vision about man's eternal quest for freedom and for self-realization.

Chapter Three

THE WESTERN AND THE INDIAN INTELLECTUALS

In the total scheme of any society in the world today the place of the intellectual has been determined by history, more particularly the history of the last five hundred years. At first glance, his function in western societies appears to be greatly different from that in the Afro-Asian societies. In the former, where almost cent per cent education prevails and the creation of most original ideas in science, technology and the humanities takes place, the intellectual stands a great distance away from the seat of political and economic power. In the latter, the intellectual himself is in the seat of power. In the intellectually developed countries, the intellectual in fact appears much more alienated from the political and economic process of development and the masses, than in the developing countries; but in actual fact, the position is the opposite.

The paradox of the situation lies in this: in the developed countries where the intellectuals stand aloof from political and administrative machinery, and have apparently no say in the framing of national and international policies, the societies are making rapid progress towards greater prosperity. In the developing countries, where the intellectuals themselves are wielding all state powers, the rate of progress is so slow as to be no progress at all.

The paradox disapears when we think of communist states in the Afro-Asian as well as European regions. In these states, the emergence of the intellectuals as rulers have certainly led to quick social prosperity. Soviet Russia in fifty years and China in twenty-five years have achieved a level of prosperity which western societies would take a hundred years to achieve. However in the communist countries, when the intellectuals acquired power, they ceased really to be intellectual and turned into ruthless, tyrannical rulers. Therefore, their coming into power resulted in the throttling of all intellectual activities except those which served the rulers.

Thus in the long run the paradox reappears in the communist states too. The intellectual, turned ruler, defeats the very purpose behind his attaining political and governmental powers. Prosperity comes at the cost of humanity itself.

Whatever the consequences, it is clear that the intellectuals in developed countries stand aloof from the administration, and also from political activities designed to capture state powers. In developing countries the intellectual is the central figure in the whole drama of power politics. Of the latter, the communist states constitute an example of an extreme nature; but this is true more or less of other Afro-Asian countries, with the exception of Japan. The situation in India provides a typical example.

Today India is ruled totally by its intellectuals, of whom a great majority are pseudo-intellectuals. Among its political leaders belonging to various parties, even the half-literate and half-educated acquire intellectual pretensions. India's bureaucracy is composed of the finest brains with great potentialities. The best among the engineering and medical students join government services. The outstanding social scientists clamour for jobs in government controlled institutes, councils and universities. Perhaps in no other country of the world does the government get such overwhelming and ready support from its intellectuals. In fact, here in India they are the government. The result cannot be called happy. The intellectual climate in India, despite its intellectuals being in power, happens paradoxically to be sterile.

How does one explain this paradoxical situation? In an attempt to answer this question, a glance at history is needed.

Even at the outset, we must distinguish between the history of Europe and that of America. From the standpoint of the role of the intellectual in social development, the distinction is markedly significant. In the making of modern Europe, the intellectual has played a vital part. He has been the harbinger and initiator of the kind of thinking which led to the renaissance, with a faith in the capacity of man to change his environment, to explore the secrets of nature and to become, in howsoever limited a sense, master of his own fate. He fought for the acceptance of his discoveries and suffered in the attempt.

In America no intellectual fight was necessary. The country enjoyed the fruits of the battle fought and won in Europe by the intellectual. America still does not have an intellectual tradition of its own, though in recent years a tradition appears to have been forming itself and throwing some tentacles in the native soil. But then, whereas modern America is only two hundred years old, modern Europe is about five hundred years old, with its intellectual tradition going back to about two thousand and five hundred years. This historical background determines the distinction between the ways in which the intellectual functions in the European and American societies.

Essentially, the beginning of the modern European intellectual tradition could be traced to the ancient Greek thinkers, Socrates, Plato and Aristotle. The Roman thinkers absorbed a good deal of the Greek thought, and later the early Christian saints and fathers absorbed much of both Greek and Roman elements into their own precepts and religion. Nevertheless, a millenium of Christian era in Europe marked a break from the early classical thinking and view of life. With the advent of the Renaissance, the revival of classical Greek learning was added to a thousand-year old tradition of christian philosophical thought and consciousness.

The discoveries of Kepler and Galileo, as well as of Newton, though inspired by faith in God, eventually led to the weakening of man's faith in God and the freeing of man's intellect from its bondage to Church superstitions. Other factors contributed to the process. Religious wars, political upheavals, the rising spirit of nationalism, the beginning of trade and commerce, discoveries of other continents and countries, to mention only a few, made a tremendous impact on the people of the time and bred in them serious doubts about a god-governed universe.

From the very beginning of the modern age in Europe, the intellectual is as much the creation of his society as the society is his creation. It is not that the intellectual led his society to social progress and economic prosperity. In Europe economic prosperity would have occurred irrespective of what the European intellectual might have contributed to it. In Britain for example, a flowering of intellectual activities has always been preceeded and never followed by, a period of great economic prosperity, brought about traders. manufacturers, seafarers and other common people of the non-intellectual class. At the best of times the European intellectual has lived through the long ordeal of social change, continuously affecting as well as being affected by it.

This harmony is disturbed in the early nineteenth century after the French Revolution, and the advent of the Romantic age in Europe. With progress of the Industrial Revolution quite a few intellectuals, still lagging behind the pace of a developing society, could not comprehend it in its entirety They flinched from the reality to escape into the colourful world of imagination.

Despite the revolt of the intellectuals, the pace of industrial progress and the modernization of social and cultural institutions continued to advance unabated. But their revolt in effect was a way of responding to the challenges of the changing society, a way of comprehending and living with them. The revolt could not have been anything but imaginative. For in the reality of every-day life the intellectuals, like others, were benefitting through concrete social and economic changes.

By the latter half of the nineteenth century the intellectuals revolt against modernization subsided, for they began to realise that its progress could not be halted. Compromises of one sort or the other between two camps were made, but a real understanding was still lacking on the part of the intellectual. This compromise was so tenuous that it shattered under the strain of the first world war. In 1918 a section of European intellectuals revolted again, though this time with a greater sense of understanding the implacable process of social change. Once again they ended up by escaping into visions of the past and of aestheticism, while the reality of social life continued to change at even a faster rate.

The second world war exploded the visions of the rebellious intellectuals. They were forced to take into account the forces of industry, commerce and technology shaping their society. This was however, the case of the literary-cultural intellectuals. As for the scientists, technologists, economists and political thinkers, they have always been working in close alliance with the common man, in a concerted attempt to modernize society.

Thus the process of development of the intellectual has been congruous with the development of the entire social order. The fruits of scientific discoveries and technological inventions, long before they became subjects of academic studies, were consumed by the common people : manufacturers, traders, merchants, government officials and so on. A few literary intellectuals of the romantic brand alienated themselves imaginatively from the inevitable historic process of social development, but a vast majority of the scientifically trained intellectuals worked assiduously along with the common people for the betterment of living conditions. For all the Goldsmiths, Wordsworths, Keats and Shelleys, or Ruskins and Carlyles and Newmans, the pace of the industrial advancement increased and transformed traditional society into a modern society. Eventually, it led to the creation of what C.P. Snow has designated as "two cultures"—one being scientific and the other literary and artistic.

Today, the European intellectual is in harmony with social and political conditions. Intellectuals do not enjoy a special category, or an exclusiveness from other people of non-intellectual profession. A natural cohesion has come to characterize the relation between the intellectual and others.

In America, the role of the intellectual in the social and economic development has been still less decisive than in Europe. The American prosperity is the result of will and drive of the masses to work, to earn and to enjoy. The bulk of the American population being immigrants from different countries of Europe, they had come to the new land with a determination to gain wealth. This was relatively easy in the fertile and virgin land with its favourable weather conditions. There was no past to look back to, and they were creators of their own history.

Even today the American intellectuals is not quite integrated into the society's economic and political system, though he enjoys its benefits. There is no doubt that intellectually too, America today is the most advanced of the western nations; but is important to remember that this intellectual advancement has followed material prosperity, not preceded it.

The Indian scene is of an altogether different nature. The

intellectual of India is not the creation of his own society. He is not the product of what we call Indian culture. He is the product of colonial rule—initially rather a by-product, but gradually becoming the chief product of the time.

This historical fact has to be reckoned with, in any attempt to consider the function of the Indian intellectuals today. Without a hundred and fifty years of the British Raj, it is anyone's guess whether the Indian intellectual would at all have existed. But, then, history is not what would have been, but what has been.

The Indian intellectual has not grown with the development of his society. He is an imposition from the top, an inevitable product of the effort of the British rulers to modernize India and educate Indians through the English medium, with a view to strengthening the foundations of the Empire. Even after the Raj, for one reason or the other, the modernizing process continued to be conducted from the top without generating a self-changing process of development. While the Indian intellectual was nursed on modern European and American thought, the society in which he lived and required to work remained almost in a primitive stage of development A hiatus was created between him and his society, and both found each other irrelevant and meaningless. This led to the stunting of intellectual power itself, and the growth of the cult of mediocrity which characterizes the Indian intellectual today.

The actual situation turned out to be worse, because at Independence the Indian intellectual attained all political power from the British ruler, without a fuller involvement of the people. The intellectual ruler ruled with ideas derived from societies which had passed through centuries of enlightened, liberal, scientific education and industrial progress—from societies with different cultural backgrounds. Plans and programes based on alien ideas, in absence of the willing involvement of the people, fell miserably short of expectations. The intellectual consequently became frustrated, desperate, confused or he became supercilious, patronizing, arrogant, snobbish, hypocritical, dictatorial.

Herein lies the crux of the problem. A healthy and prosperous society has never been built by intellectuals or, worse still, men with intellectual pretensions. The intellectual-ruled society tends to be authoritarian and ultimately anti-intellectual. The healthy growth of a society depends upon the involvement of the masses in the development of various processes. This involvement can be real and productive only when such a social system is devised which induces the masses to work voluntarily for their own enrichment which, in effect, is the enrichment of all society. Such a social system cannot be imposed from without; it has to evolve from within. The intellectual in power is not likely to let such a social system evolve, for the pace of such an evolutionary system is necessarily somewhat slower, though more fundamental, and the intellectual grows easily impatient. He is much too anxious to prove his worth to the masses and win their laurels, by achieving something quick, no matter how superficial and self-defeating in the long run that might be.

Chapter Four

IN SEARCH OF AN INDIAN TRADITION

In India, by tradition we mean generally a heritage of the past. To be traditional is to reverse to the past, to accept it in a spirit of veneration. There is no room for criticism and evualuation. In fact, criticism is strictly forbidden. Naturally, this leads to a glorification of the past.

The larger and more creative sense of tradition has never been accepted here. It is still unacceptable indeed, though not in word. In this sense, tradition is not a transference of the past values to the present world, nor is it the present world's clinging to the past when social conditions and economic relations have undergone a vast change. In this true sense, tradition is a continuity of the past as modified by the present. A heathy tradition is never afraid of modification through criticism and assessment, in the light of new knowledge. In fact, the more a tradition is subjected to criticism, the tougher and healthier it becomes.

Such a tradition characterizes the development of European society, from early Greek and Roman times through the Middle Ages to the present time. There has never been a total break with the past. Christianity retained quite a few barbaric rituals, and the Renaissance, while reviving Greek and Roman thought, retained much of essential Christian thought. With the Industrial Revolution the past was subjected to severe criticism, reassessment and modification. Every step forward on the way to social and economic progress was accompanied by an adjustment with the past, and every adjustment was a re-creation of the past. Even today in the space-age of European thought, Plato and Aristotle are latent influences.

Tradition is essentially a matter of an attitude to life, a bent of mind, a way of apprehending the world and the universe, and a way of approaching human and social relationships. A continuity of these intellectual and emotional characteristics in people is the essence of tradition. With the progress of science and technology social conditions might change beyond recognition, but tradition might still remain alive in the way of thinking and looking at the world. In this sense European society is still traditional, and the American society is not.

Is there any such Indian intellectual tradition ? There is, and there is not. Evidently, there is one which is suggested by the phrase however vague, "the Indian way of looking at things." There is not in the sense that "the Indian way" is not intellectual by nature.

Ancient Indian history is largely an imaginative restructuring of the long past, on the basis of available fragments of record. Certain things immediately relevant to the intellectual life of those days are clear. First, throughout the *Vedic* age, a glorious age of intellectual achievement, the only means of communication was oral. The first written script is said to have come into use towards the end of King Asoka's reign. By that time the *Vedas* had been in oral existence for over 1000 years or so. Even after the invention of scripts, many centuries lapsed before the *Vedas* were written. Even after they were written, they continued to be passed on orally from one generation to the other. The tradition is still alive in certain orthodox sections of the Hindu community.

Now, from the point of view of intellectual development, the prevalence of the oral tradition in India has had a serious drawback. It did not encourage intellectual curiosity, a desire to understand and analyze and improve upon the given material. The oral transmission of songs is a different matter. But the transmission of the available esoteric knowledge led to the exclusive status of the teacher, the *guru*, and the *pandit*, that is the Brahmin with the memorized knowledge of the *Vedas*. The word of the *pandit* carried an authority which others could not challenge.

Similarly, no disciple, or *chela*, had the right to question the word of his teacher. The disciple had to submit himself wholly to his teacher and the latter would treat his ward

patronisingly. The relationship between the two and the
quality of teaching in the circumstances depended upon the
personal character of both the *guru* and the *chela*. It was
common practice that the *guru* would not impart all his knowledge to the *chela*. He must keep certain essential things to
himself. The idea evidently was to keep the *chela* always a
chela, never allowing him to become as great as the *guru* or be
able to challenge the *guru*.

This tradition continues even today, among the Indian
teachers and educationists, though in a highly refined form.
A university professor in India has retained the essential
attitude of the ancient *guru*. Knowledge, or whatever knowledge he has, can no longer be kept from his *chelas* since it has
got to be written; but he still demands from them personal
loyalty and obedience characteristic of the old *guru*. From
this traditional attitude has originated cliques and groups in
the Indian educational institutions. While groups are condemned, the personal loyalty of the *chelas* to the *gurus* is still
upheld as an ideal, since it is traditional.

This is clearly an anti-intellectual element in the Indian
cultural and intellectual tradition. It prevents a student or a
young teacher from approching ideas objectively. To become
loyal, so to say, to the ideas and not to the *guru*, he becomes
more preoccupied with showing his loyalty to the *guru* than
with sifting the ideas which his *guru* has imparted to him.

The continuation of the oral tradition has adversely affected
the intellectual development in another way. It has bred a
tendency to regard the word of the teacher as final, and not
to investigate in any further. This has continued even after the
written word came in use. It is not surprising that adequate
critical commentaries on the *Vedas* or *Gita* have never been
written till very recent times, and that too by way only of
academic excercises. Even such a social document as *Manu-
smriti* has been taken as final and beyond any critical appraisal.
By the time Kautilya came to formulate his political and
economic ideas in his *Arthasastra,* the written script had
come into vogue; but no critical document dealing with *Artha-
sastras*, written then or even much later, is available.

Today, when the written word has come to acquire the
authority which the oral word had earlier, the same traditional

attitude makes the Indian intellectual accept it as the final word on the subject. This explains way Indian intellectuals in the univerisites are not writing original books at all. They are largely satisfied with interpreting the texts written, and upheld as authoritative elsewhere. What the *Vedas* were to them in the distant past, the European-American books are to them at present. Their business is to explain them, interpret them, but never to subject them to criticism. No doubt other cultural factors have contributed to this tendency, but the uncritical intellectual tradition has affected it a lot.

This is partly why in India there never has been anything like an intellectual community which gets formed through the objective pursuit of knowledge. From ancient times we have had individual seers, scholars prophets, of great excellence but from none of them has emanated a school of learning and thought. They did not initiate a community of seekers of knowledge, each pursuing it freely and objectively, taking nothing for granted. The *gurus* themselves would see to it that such a community does not grow.

The result of such a deep seated cultural trait has been disastrous for the growth of intellectual life in India. The knowledge which the *guru* withheld from his *chelas* died with his death. Even that knowledge which he had imparted tended to decay after his death, since the *chelas* were loyal to him personally and not to his ideas. And when one of the *chelas* would became a *guru*, he would claim to have known everything originally, and make his own *chelas* in-turn.

Closely allied to it is another traditional Indian belief, that knowledge cannot be produced through systematic observation and logical reasoning. For one thing, a traditional Indian thinks that all knowledge for all time lies in the *Vedas* and other scriptures. There can be no thing beyond them. If there is, it is only false, deceptive and self-destructive. The eternal knowled is stored up in the various scriptures. To follow them in whatever way one can is to follow the truth. For the knowledge contained in the *Vedas* and other scriptures is in reality directly derived from God, and no man can improve upon it. From this comes the traditional belief that no man can acquire knowledge without the blessings of God, or of the *guru* who carries the word of God. Endeavouring to acquire knowledge would be fruitless, unless the learner is God's favourite child or the *guru's* favourite disciple.

Since all knowledge is contained in the *Vedas*, acquiring knowledge meant knowing the *Vedas*. That was considered the real and the highest knowledge, and knowledge of any other thing was inferior and not worth striving after. In fact, the ancient Indian believed, and the traditional Indian still believes, that the knowledge contained in the *Vedas* was not really knowledge as such, but something beyond knowledge. Knowledge was acquired through perception and analytical faculty of the intellect, but the *Vedas* were beyond perception and intellect. They belonged to the world of intuition, of supra-intellectual, purely spiritual apprehension. Thus knowledge gained through intellectual reasoning is of an inferior type, useful in the limited material sense, but not in the ultimate spiritual sense.

This explains partly why the Indian intellectual is so readily drawn to any one discrediting knowledge gained through reasoning and upholding supra-intellectual, intuitive knowledge gained through moments of sudden spritual illumination. For this reason, most university professors, journalists and lawyers are drawn to Aurobindo's Ashram in Pondichery, or to Satya Sri Sai Baba, or even to Maharishi Mahesh Yogi and his tribe. Because of this deep seated inclination in the Indian intellectuals, even such a cult as the Ananda Marg is said to have claimed the discipleship of university teachers.

All this offers at least a partial explanation for the complacency in the Indian intellectual life, and its indifference towards acquiring and contributing to empirical knowledge about the world and its forms of life. The inner cultural urge is lacking.

With the Muslim invasion from about 900 A.D., the Hindu intellectual life withdrew further into its shell of traditional attitudes. The rise of Buddhism did not pose a serious threat to Hinduism. At any rate Buddhism was a sort of intellectual extension of some core aspects of Hinduism, but it was under the aegis of Buddhism that the first educational institutions resembling a university were established at Nalanda and Takshila. Later on, the followers of Jainism propounded by Lord Mahavira Tirthankara were again an offshoot of Hinduism, Even Sikhism, as enunciated in the *Gurugranth*, is basically a Hindu faith. Had all these offshoots continued to flourish freely in the next few centuries, Hinduism certainly would have altogether became richer with intellectual fruits culled from its outgrowths.

With the beginning of Muslim invasions, the first to fall victim to their swords were the Buddhists, who were easily recognizable by their dress and appearance, and who had raised monumental educational and intellectual centres throughout north-east India. With the disappearance of Buddhists and the gradual occupation of India by Muslim raiders, the Hindus turned more rigid and intransigent in their attitude to life and withdrew more and more to their traditional rituals. While the traditional Hindu religious-cultural tradition thrived almost intact, its more intellectually-inclined offshoot of Buddhism came to be totally destroyed from the country of its origin.

By the time the Mughals came to establish their empire in the north and north-east India, Hindu cultural life had shrunk to a body of taboos and a bundle of superstitious rituals, thereby destroying any prospect of or scope for intellectual activity. Increasingly the intellectuals withdrew from political and social life and conducted themselves well to aquire glory in the other world, to which their souls would be transported after death.

The picture changed somewhat as the Mughal empire matured under Akbar's reign. He tried to induce a certain amount of cultural exchange by marrying Hindu women and giving them total religious freedom; by founding a new religion, called the *Dini Ilahi*, compounded of both Hindu and Muslim religious essences; by employing Hindus as administrators and army commanders ; and by allowing freedom of worship to all. As a result of this liberalization there arose certain liberal Hindu reformers, poets and preachers. Even so, the Hindus never came out in the open, remaining ensconced in their shell of traditional thought. Not long afterwards the whole political policy of Akbar was reversed by Aurangzeb, and the Hindus resumed their intransigence.

A long contact with the Muslim culture through the Mughal empire did induce Hindus to become acquainted with an entirely different cultural and intellectual life, and make the necessary adjustment since it had come to stay. In this adjustment, their traditional culture was a great help.

Contrary to general opinion, the Hindus do not look down upon the world they live in. To them, this world is important in so for as it nurses the body, the house of the soul, the *atman*, the spark of the divine. Protection of one's body, one's life under any circumstance is religiously enjoined upon the Hindus. *Atman rakshito dharma*—is stipulated in the scriptures. For the protection of one's life in this world, one can adopt any means, even those which are irreligious or sinful. It is necessary to live a full life span, to perform the religious rituals to ensure that in the next birth one is born a Hindu. With this end in view, whatever he does will have no impact upon his religious spiritual life. The two worlds—worldly and the spiritual—stand apart, completely independent of each other. Deeds performed in the one have consequences limited to it alone. One may turn into a thief or robber for maintaining himself, but he may still be a religious man by performing the prescribed religious rituals in his personal life. *Ravana*, the demon-king, of the *Ramayana*, is a mythical illustration of this. He is said to be sinful in wordly activities but a great *pandit* and practitioner of religious rituals. In the end he is killed at the hand of God and attains *moksha*.

During the Mughal period, therefore, a large number of Hindus came to learn Urdu and join the administrative service. They worked with or for Muslims, for the sake of protecting their *atman* in the present world, to remain alive and enjoy the pleasures of this life. Their contacts with the Muslims remained confined to the areas of worldly life. As for their intellectual life, which to them was no different from the spiritual life, they always fell back upon the *Vedic* rituals, the philosophy of the *Gita*, and the epics of the *Ramayana* and the *Mahabharta*.

Nevertheless a widening of sensibility, howsoever slight, did take place as a result of the contact with Muslims. Once the Hindus learnt Urdu, it was natural for them to get acquainted with the romantic Urdu literature. They were introduced for the first time to certain refinements of sentiment, courtesies in behaviour and aesthetic pleasures involved in man-woman relationships. While this gave a much needed inducement to the writing of the earlier secular literature, the intellectual life remained totally unaffected. For Muslim culture itself was devoid of much intellectual content. It was basically a culture of warriors and knights, based on sentimental love and sex and on idolized heroism. The Muslim emperors who exemplified the culture, surrounded themselves with flatterers, and they did not encourage free intellectual enquiry. No doubt there were potential intellectuals among the courtiers, but since the emperors were not interested in intellectual discussions, except for the sake of diversion, pretension, or, again, recreation, the possibility was used up by devising ways and means of pleasing the emperors. Nothing worth mentioning as achievement in the intellectual life was produced during the long period of the Mughal empire.

Chapter Five

THE QUESTION OF IDENTITY

The question of identity is admittedly a complex one which touches upon and is related to the various aspects of man living in society. There are different kinds of identity—individual, political, religious, social and national—none of which can really be fully understood in isolation of others. And basically identity of any kind emanates from history, from the sufferings and joys, struggles and achievements, as well as failures, of people through centuries, both individually and socially. But history by itself does not award identity to a society, as merely being alive gives no identity to an individual. Identity is always created. Identity is always earned.

From the point of view of intellectual activity, however, the question of national identity is of cardinal importance. Of course, the sense of national identity itself is largely the creation of the intellectual, but the existence of a political-social identity must necessarily precede it. Political freedom is an indispensable precondition for the fruitful activities of the intellectual which, carried on with a sense of definite direction through years and years, eventually help create national identity. In England this sense emerged during the early symptoms of the Renaissance, but became strengthened and pervasive through the years of great intellectual flowering and social turbulence in the sixteenth and seventeenth centuries. In America, political freedom was won over two hundred years ago, but national identity began to emerge only since the first world war or so. Even today, the intellectual quest for and the creation of national identity continues in America, for this identity has to be preserved and enriched with perseverance and hard work.

The case of national identity in India is not so much complex as confused. Even a cursory glance at the history of India, with a view to tracing the growth and nature of identity, reveals the confusion created by different rulers and their lackey-historians. The debris collected by them still blocks the view of the reality that was and, consequently, the reality that is.

Certain important facts, however, clearly stand out. Of overwhelming importance among them is the fact of India being made into one administrative unit for the first time, under British rule. This had never happened before: a vast subcontinent, big enough to contain almost all Europe, was being administered from one centre, with laws applicable and enforced. This made an impact, both salubrious and deleterious, of far-reaching significance on the Indian mind.

Before the British the Muslim rule in India was of a perfunctory nature. Until the establishment of the Mughal Empire, the Muslim rulers regarded India as their conquered territory and exploited its riches mercilessly. To them India remained an alien land, and they often returned with the spoils to their own countries. Although after their return some of their army commanders stayed on and conquered fresh territories, they too never treated India as their homeland.

The Mughal rulers beginning with Babar were different in this respect. They had come to stay in India as rulers, not marauders. After Babar stabilized the kingdom, the later kings from Humayun onward implemented some social welfare schemes. They devised a loose framework of a legal system (though the king's word was always the law), and encouraged some programs of cultural harmony with the native Hindus. Nevertheless, excepting during the region of Akbar and also Jehangir, the Mughal rule could not settle down securely on Indian soil. The frontiers of the kingdom remained confined mostly to north India, and even there they were always uneasy.

Yet the Mughal administration was an advance on the situation before. Excepting perhaps Asoka, more than a thousand centuries ago, no Hindu ruler had established his hegemony over such vast areas as the Mughal kings. The Hindu period of Indian history is characterized by fragmentation, intercine quarrels, useless battles, vain pride, weak administration and an effeminate army equipped with outdated weapons. The Mughal kings tried to put together the fragments of Hindu kingdoms scattered all over the country under one administration and they achieved a fair measure of success. But the south, particularly Maharashtra, always defied the established authority of the Mughals, and even in the north the kings had to be ever prepared to meet the challenges, sometimes serious ones, thrown by rebellious groups of people. They never really were allowed to live in peace for a long time to think of other things than their own pleasures. In any case, such an empire was not destined to last long, though Aurangzeb hastened considerably the process of its disintegration. Any thought about what would have happened after the death of Aurangzeb, had the Britishers not arrived on the scene just then makes one shudder, for the thought leads to wild guesses which, of course, are of no consequence.

With the establishment of the British Raj, the Indian subcontinent came under one government, which ruled much more securely and more peacefully than ever before. The Raj had tamed both the Hindus and the Muslims to peaceful coexistence throughout the length and breadth of the country, and both the communities behaved well, if somewhat obsequiously. What had never been achieved before became a reality under the Raj: the whole of India became one administrative and political unit.

How had this come about? Why was there no considerable resistance to the British rule for about a century or so? The reason is not really what is popularly believed in: the overwhelming superiority of the British army in the battlefield, because of its great skill in warfare and equipment. This may be the reason for victorious wars and establishment of the Raj, but not for its relatively peaceful and fruitful continuance for such a long period.

The real reason was the superiority of the rulers, in respect to governance. They certainly ruled as masters, though not as kings, but they ruled methodically in accordance with a system. The notion that justice is indivisible, that it does not depend upon the whim of rulers, was first introduced in actual administration by the British. This in itself had a revolutionary effect upon the natives of all communities, for centuries used to the rule of the rod. Here was the first real initiation to democracy, a system totally foreign to Indian culture, both Hindu and Muslim. People felt liberated from the bondage to kings and rulers, and allied themselves happily with the new judiciary system which applied to both rulers and the ruled alike.

This was supported by the introduction of modern education in India. The first three universities of India at Calcutta, Bombay and Madras were founded as early as in 1858-59, with English as the medium of education. This was another factor of deep and far-reaching significance. It opened up to the Indians a vast world of knowledge based on practical reasoning and empiricism, and the systematic observation of concrete life around. It bound the far-flung corners of India under one educational system of a liberal and secular nation, and with one common language.

Then came the railways and the motor vehicles, helping quick and easy mobility and the transport of goods from one part of the vast land to the other. With more and more people of different corners learning the one common language of English, communication on an all-India level was fast becoming a possibility. Through newly formed newspapers and journals, fresh and modern ideas started impinging upon the Indian mind. The modern age of India had begun.

Out of these changes emerged the idea of India as being one land, with all the people living there as identified with it. A country composed of different communities was united under the British rule under one administrative, judiciary and educational system. True, the British rulers did not intend it consciously to happen. It happened inadvertently. A country was born, but it had to acquire nationhood.

Perhaps it was the quest for nationhood that primarily urged the great social and religious reformers of the late nineteenth century. Euphemistically the period has been called the age of renaissance. So it was, in a limited sense of the term. The new awakening was confined to educational, social and religious aspects of life. Later on, towards the end of the century and the beginning of the twentieth, the awakening also aroused political aspirations of the educated Indian, imbued by then with western liberal ideas. But the quest for national identity by a people still under foreign rule cannot be real. The real quest can begin only after complete political freedom.

Nevertheless, an awakening did take place, inspired by a desire to seek a national identity. It would be helpful to examine the nature of this awakening, for it conditioned the character of both the Indian intellectual and the Indian freedom movement.

In the first place, the awakening had come clearly in consequence of the liberal higher education in the English medium. This is of course a well-known fact, but the seminal impact of it on the Indian intellectual is often underrated. It exposed the Indian educated mind to the vast exciting world of modern knowledge, and the sensitive ones were liberated from their servile bondage to their primitive tenets of traditional faith. Between Macaulay's historic Minute in response to Raja Ram Mohan Roy's passionate appeal for the introduction of English, and the founding of the Indian National Congress, is the period of fertilization of the Indian mind with European thought, through English education. The flowering of the Indian mind, impregnated with modern thought, begins to manifest itself from the early eighties onward. First came the religious reformers, sifting the essential tenets of Hindu religion from its superstitious, ritualistic outgrowths. Most of them, like Vivekananda, spoke in English and re-stated the essence of the religion in modern idiom, re-assessed it on principles of logic, and took it beyond the frontiers of the country to Europe and America.

Within the country itself, for the first time, the words of the religious reformers could be conveyed in one common language, that is in English. The idea itself, that the whole of what was even then India had essentially one religious culture and social outlook, emerged much more convincingly than ever before, through the use of English. Through English, it would be true to say, India was rediscovered.

It is significant that in this first phase of the intellectual-cultural awakening, the Muslims of India played no part at all. In fact they could have done nothing at that stage, for in the rediscovery of India's long history they could share only a few centuries. Therefore during this phase the Muslims kept aloof from the awakening. Nor is there any evidence that, like Hindu religious reformers, the Muslims made any attempt at modernizing their religious practices. In fact, for quite a long time, the Muslims did not take to English education as enthusiastically as the Hindus, or to modern liberal ideas from Europe. The memory of their being members of the ruling community was still undimmed in their minds and they hated any association with the English people who had usurped their power to rule.

It must be noted that this awakening was strictly limited to the newly educated class, and that a large number of them were not even affected deeply or even genuinely. They took to English educational primarily to get jobs, and not all of them paid much thought to the reforming of their religion. They became indifferent to religious matters and anxious to live the modern way. Thus the first fruition of the renaissance was severely limited in appeal. In fact, its impact did not go beyond the big cities and towns, Indian villages remained almost totally unaffected by the renaissance, which included over ninety-five percent of the Indian population, both Hindu and Muslim, living on with their old traditional beliefs. To most of them even the concept of a country was foreign, and the notion of reforming religion wholly absurd, if not sacrilegious.

The same pattern of relationship between a handful of English-educated intellectuals and the rest of the people continued till the early years of the present century. The founding of the Indian National Congress in 1885 too was merely an act of the newly educated intellectuals, and that too under the leadership of an Englishman, A.O. Hume. The purpose behind the Congress then was not to demand freedom but to cooperate with the British rulers, with a view to democratizing the administration. The earliest members of the Congress were drawn from an anglocised aristocratic class, highly educated, most of them in Britain, and inspired by the ideas of the British social thinkers.

It was then that the Muslims in the cities began to come forward and acquire an English education. Sharing in the ruling administration was after all next best to be the rulers of the land. They certainly smelt the political opportunities of the future. In fact, it was with the rise of Muslims and their joining the Congress that the latter tended to be politicized.

And with this also set in the first symptoms, though not noticed at the time, of the confusion in national identity. Which India was to be accepted for purposes of determining a national identity: the one that the Hindu social-religious reformers rediscovered through the study of the ancient history, or the other of the recent past, which belonged to the Muslims? These two pasts were not easily reconcilable without compromise. This confusion, created by inherent historical incongruity, increased with the Congress acquiring the character of a political party, and came to the surface as soon as demand for political independence was openly voiced.

From the standpoint of attaining a national identity and the full flowering of India's intellectual potential, the call for political freedom was perhaps immature. For this inevitably released the forces of chauvinism, revivalism, the glorification of obscurantism, even fanaticism, which deflected and diffused the process of modernization, howsoever gradual, being conducted by the British rulers. The demand for political freedom had to be buttressed with arousing people's pride in the country's past, which contained the seeds of dissension. At that immature stage of the fitful modernization of social life, when only about ten percent of urban population had received modern education but had not wholly developed a modern outlook, an appeal to the kind of past India had was bound to lead to self-contradictory tendencies. Once the modernizing process covered larger sections of society, including the rural, when education had become more wide-spread and people in general had acquired forward-looking, scientific attitudes to problems of life, there would have been no need to appeal passionately to the past, in order to enlist people's support.

But this was not to be. Ironically enough, this was due to the impatience and short-sightedness of the aristocratic English-educated intellectuals. On the one hand, they came to be deeply inspired by thinkers like Burke, Locke Rousseau, Goethe, Carlyle, Ruskin, Shaw, Tolstoy and others to demand their freedom. On the other, they were tempted gradually away from cooperating with the rulers, to wish to take over the whole charge of administration itself. This was not possible without political freedom, which was not possible without evincing popular support; which, in turn, was not possible without arousing their pride in what they were in the past, and shame in what they had come to be in the present.

Under the circumstances, the question of discovering a national identity had to be answered in the vaguest possible terms. Since the intellectuals were themselves also leaders, they had to use a camouflage of high-sounding, awe-inspiring words, to arouse the people and impress the rulers. Apparently, in this exercise both Hindu and Muslim intellectuals joined hands together, in both swearing by modern secular democratic ideals in which, perhaps, they themselves did believe, but of which the people, 95 percent of them, had not heard. They could be stirred only by appealing to the past, and this became the principle.

This dilemma characterizes the intellectual activities at that period of Indian history—a dilemma which was not resolved through the freedom struggle. On the contrary, it worsened gradually and then, precipitously just before Independence, until it reached a compromised resolution in the clumsy act of partition.

Chapter Six

THE PROMISE OF THE FREEDOM STRUGGLE

One of the unique features of the Indian freedom struggle was that it was conducted and carried on wholly by intellectuals and educated men and women. The masses did not participate in it in any considerable number, at least till Mahatma Gandhi returned from South Africa and launched his programs of mass movement. Even after that, it is debatable whether more than fifteen per cent of the population ever took part in any of Gandhi's satyagraha movements; and out of them how many were clear in their mind about the political objectives in view.

It will be remembered that even Gandhi's following constituted largely of highly educated men and women, primarily of the urban areas. People of the rural areas were attracted to Gandhi more by a sense of awe than by any clear notion of what Gandhi stood for. They followed Gandhi as they would follow a religious saint and not a political leader, a character about whom they had never heard. Gandhi knew this, he himself being one of the shrewdest intellectuals of his time. His appeal for participation in his movement was always directed to intellectuals: teachers, students, lawyers, bureaucrats and others. Though Gandhi's prayer meetings and political meetings drew huge crowds, among his closest lieutenants were distinguished intellectuals in the country: Rajendra Prasad, Jayprakash Narayan, Jawaharlal Nehru, Mahadeo Desai, Pyarelal, Kaka Kalelkar, to name only a few. Among his friends were great world intellectuals such as Tolstoy, Romain Rolland, C.F. Andrews and others.

Since the lives of the Indian semi-urban and rural masses were never allowed to influence the intellectuallzed freedom struggle, theoretical and conceptual aspects of the problems dominated the deliberations of the intellectual-political leaders. Even when the people from the Indian villages joined the freedom movement, nearly 80 percent of them were educated. Consequently, much of the political discussion was abstract and polemical in character. The persistent demand was, in the first phase, for a share in administration and, in the second phase for the complete transfer of administrative and political power. Intellectually inspired as the leaders were by political thinkers and political movements in the world, they wished to shape Indian life each in accordance with his dream. Throughout the period of the struggle, they did not think it necessary to prepare the masses for the great responsibility of political freedom. This was a gigantic task which Gandhi almost alone tried to accomplish in his own manner, in a relatively extremely short time. The masses could not be ignored; but they must be used as followers, almost blind followers, by the intellectual-political leaders.

In these circumstances, the question of national identity could not always have been ignored in political discussions. Whenever the question popped up, it was hastily tucked under the carpet of improvised, compromising, interpretations. Undoubtedly, as the Congress leaders started making demands for full political freedom, the question vexed the Muslim intellectual-political leaders more than the Hindu leaders and intellectuals. The intellectual activities of the Hindus was infinitely richer and more varied than of the Muslims, mainly because the former had become fully conscious beyond doubt of their national identity while the Muslims were still groping. By comparison the Muslim intellectuals felt inhibited and unsure, and therefore their achievements during this period are of routine, academic nature. The confusion of national identity befogged their creative spirit.

The great awakening naturally took place among the Hindu intellectuals outside politics. In the beginning, in the last decade of the nineteenth and the first two decades of the twentieth century, the intellectuals were stirred to creativity by a new awareness of the past gained through modern education. Later on they were inspired by the Gandhian movement, and the idea and prospect of political freedom.

A notable feature of this great awakening was that it began in the big cities with modern universities, such as Calcutta, Bombay and Madras, and with highly educated intellectuals. In Bengal the renaissance writers such as Bankim Chandra, Sarat Chandra and, later on Tagore, developed from their study of English thought and literature. Bankim Chandra was initially so fascinated by the English language that he is known to have written his first novel in English.

In comparison with Madras and Bombay, Calcutta had a much larger share of intellectuals in the first phase of the renaissance intellectuals. The reason was obviously that Calcutta was then the capital of the British India and consequently, its intellectuals were in closer touch with the British people, their civilization and culture. This also affected the character of the literature and ideas produced in Bengal, as distinguished from those of Madras and Bombay. While Bengali literature and thought was modern in character and showed an awareness of modern European psychology and philosophy, Tamil and Marathi literatures of that period were imbued with the traditional spirit. Even in Bengali literature, the spirit of tradition was itself perceived through and modified in the light of modern knowledge.

Out of this awakening were obtained the richest harvest of Indian intellectual activities, particularly between the years 1910 and 1935. Jagdish Chandra Bose, C.V. Raman, Rabindranath Tagore earned international fame for their towering achievements in science and literature. They put India on the world map of intellectuals, and prepared the ground for a fuller and wider intellectual flowering in a country teeming with millions of people. Indeed, for a time India produced outstanding figures in mathematics, physics, chemistry, biology, economics, history, philosophy and literature. Indian academicians earned a place for themselves in world scholarship. The genius of the Indian mind, it seemed, was fully awakening after thousands of years.

By this time education in English had become fairly widespread in the country. Schools and colleges with the English medium had been established throughout the country and more and more people of all communities were taking to a liberal English education. The primary objective of course, in the case of most people, was to get jobs in the fast expanding government offices. Secondarily, they were also tempted to be come acquainted with the knowledge that had produced the railways, the automobiles, the aeroplanes, the astounding weapons of war, the complex administrative machinery, the judiciary and so on. In the case of those who came from rich feudalistic, upper-class families, the primary objective behind acquiring this education was not the government jobs but the modern knowledge and style of modern living, in order to retain their superior position in society. By 1925-30 English had become the medium of instruction at colleges and high schools throughout India. Even in village primary schools, education started with the first book of the English alphabet.

The result was the growth of an increasing number of people with modern education, ready to acquire higher modern knowledge and give up their traditional beliefs. Indian society was poised for the modernization of thought and conditions of living. The unity of India seemed axiomatic, since the entire country through newspapers and periodicals and books was speaking in one language and in one voice.

It is true that English was that one language, but it must also be seen that the use of English did not in any way prevent the growth of the regional languages. On the contrary, it helped fundamentally in their growth and development. The reason why Bengali language and literature flourished to such excellences during this period was the close association of the writers with English literature and European thought. The same explanation applies to the making of the Tamil and Marathi literatures. It was a peculiarly enriching and fruitful phenomenon. The writers of the period were not overwhelmed or inhibited by the vastness of English literature or the depth and profundity of European thought. They avidly read foreign literature to become more acutely aware of their own cultural and literary heritage, to be induced to reinterpret them in terms of modern experience, and to express themselves in their own languages. Unlike writers of the post-independence period, those of the pre-independence days, particularly of the first four decades of the twentieth century, were never imitators of the western literary movements. They imbibed western thought through English, felt exhilarated by the new experience and expressed it all in their own native language. The very need of writing in one's own language was felt as a result of becoming familiar with different literature in Europe through English translations. The writers enriched their regional languages in the sense that they made them, or tried to make them, a fit medium for literary expression of modern experience.

English naturally came to acquire total supremacy, both as medium of instruction and as a medium of communication in non-literary subjects. Thus was because the regional languages from the point of view of scientific-intellectual content and capability, were still in an undeveloped position. Yet even in this field of ideas and intellectual discussion, the first steps to improve regional languages had already been taken during those days. In primary as well as high schools, as also in many colleges, instruction in social sciences began to be given through regional languages. No one at that time could have dreamt of the enmity ever developing between English and the regional languages, or among the regional languages themselves. Had the process gone on for a longer period undisturbed by extraneous exigencies, it would ultimately have resulted in the greater enrichment and an all-round development of the regional languages as adequate media of both literary and non-literary intellectual activities.

The first schism however, appears soon after Tilak's declaration, "Complete self-rule is our birth-right" and Gandhi's implementation of his mass-movement programs. This was however, limited to the schism between English on the one hand and the regional languages on the other. After independence, enmity would develop also between one regional language and the other, but not during the period of freedom struggle. At that time, it came to be English versus the Indian languages. While this served the political end of the Congress leaders, it introduced seeds of confusion which have not yet been totally weeded out.

An appeal to arouse the people to support the Congress demand for self-rule had to be made through the Indian languages, which the masses could follow. Whatever the consequences later, in the beginning the stress on studying and working in the Indian languages, particularly in Hindi, resulted in a spurt of significant intellectual activity, especially in literature. The stalwarts of Hindi language, at that time enjoying indisputably the veneration of all as the future national language, were produced during this period of history. Premchand was never to be excelled in the field of novel, Nirala in poetry, and Agyeya as an all-round experimentalist. As a literary critic and historian, Ramchandra Shukla has yet to be surpassed.

Again it was during this period that what is now called Indo-Anglian literature had its beginning and, what is more, reached a point of excellence to which it has never been able to come up since then. Mulk Raj Anand and Raja Rao had written their best novels between 1930 and 1946, and R.K. Narayan too had published the best of his early works during this period. Although after independence, more Indians from all corners of India were to write novels in English, none of them would deserve to be placed anywhere near these three pioneers. The story of Indo-Anglian poetry is however, of a different kind. Fewer poets appeared then of limited scope, but hundreds of poets afterwards, quite a few of them attaining remarkables levels of excellence. From Sarojini Naidu to Nissim Ezekiel is a long way indeed.

Invariably two intellectual ideas current at that time influenced the release of creative energy, both emanating from the Congress leadership with Gandhi as the father-figure. They were the idea of independence and the idea of secular democracy, as professed by the Congress. In fact the most dominating idea of Independence was inseparable from Gandhi and his program of action. Consequently Gandhi was the seed which fertilized the creative minds in different languages. He provided the whole context: philosophical, social, moral, ethical, religious, political, economic, all in one. He came to be perceived by these writers as the modern embodiment of India's ancient glories, and he dominated the Indian political, intellectual and social scene like a colossus.

The extent of Gandhi's domination can easily be seen from what his presence did to other political parties such as the Communist Party and the Socialist Party, both as thoroughly intellectual in character as the Congress. There was the Hindu Mahasabha too, a party of militant, traditional Hindu intellectuals. Last but not the least was the Muslim League, a party of the militant Muslim intellectuals. None of these parties, however, could publicly defy or oppose Gandhi, since Gandhi's congress was made up of all those elements of which separately each party was composed. In addition, it had something which no other party actually had: mass appeal and mass contact, which was the big contribution of Gandhi's personality.

The intellectual leaders of other political parties derived their ideas of revolution, freedom and socialism from currents of thought in foreign countries or in ancient India, and spent a major part of their time and energy in hair-splitting as to what really was what. Nearly all the leaders of the parties including the Congress were English educated, and, invariably, the topmost ones were educated and trained in foreign countries, particularly in England and America. As intellectuals they were bristling with ideas culled from Rousseau, Ruskin, de Tocqueville, Emerson, Laski, Marx and Engels and Lenin. Yet they lacked the inclination, because they were intellectuals, to instil them into the masses and prepare them for a mass revolution, for here, they knew, Gandhi had already stolen the show. The "revolutionary" intellectual leaders thought that the masses were too traditional to be stirred to participate in any modern revolution. The "traditional" intellectuals were plagued by doubts, whether the masses having lived in the modern social conditions, would respond to their call for reverting to the traditional outlook. Gandhi combined in himself and his programs both the extremes: leftism and rightism, and modernism and traditionalism, which, indeed cut across all intellectual "isms." Besides, Gandhi assumed an appearance and a *modus operandi* which appealed strongly to the idealistic-minded Indian people. In view of the tremendous Gandhian appeal, all other political parties, except the communist party, the policy of which was guided less by national than international (particularly Russian) considerations, chose to eschew their differences with the Congress. At least for the time being, they fought together with Congress for the cause of political freedom.

As for Gandhi's influence on the intellectuals of the country, it was, to say the least, extremely complex and ambiguous. During the period under discussion this was not noticeable, for it was drowned under the crowding political developments concerned with the immediate goal of achieving freedom.

On the one hand, the advent of Gandhi provided a philosophical-social context necessary for the flowering of literature, the arts and the sciences. An appearance of national identity too seemed to be growing out of the personality and the programs of Gandhi. The result was a rich harvest of what appeared to be the first crop of intellectual achievements, with promises of richer harvest.

On the other hand, Gandhi in his bid to compromise with extreme views and resolve the social contradictions, tended to create confusion of a kind. Hence the total dependence on him, of even such Congress intrellectuals as Jawaharlal Nehru, Maulana Azad and Rajendra Prasad. The confusion, essentially speaking, continued to block the intellectual's view of reality ever afterwards.

Let us take two fundamental aspects of Gandhian social outlook: modernism versus traditionalism, and religiosity versus secularism. On both counts, his views and his practices were anachronistic and backward rather than forward-looking, though apparently he would claim to be against neither modernism nor secularism. As a political weapon, as an instrument of gaining mass support, the camouflage worked excellently to the desired effect; but it led to a confusion of national directions in the practical objectives of social reconstruction. Out of this confusion was created the scope for hypocrisy, pretension and evasion. The *charkha*, for example, was extremely effective in arousing the mass-consciousness for freedom and a spirit of self-reliance, during the pre-independence period. To establish it as the ideal economic objective was highly impractical in a country where modern textile mills had already come into existence, where people were taking to mill-made clothes, national or foreign.

Where is the *charkha* today? Nowhere in the lives of the people. But as an ideal it still exists and often attracts the intellectuals to discuss its relevance. As an ideal it has created confusion when those evidently professing to live upto it have simultaneously subscribed to values incoherent with the *khadhi* They spun *charkha* and wore *khadhi*, but they lived in palatial buildings with a fleet of cars and servants, used all modern technology and feasted on sumptuous food. This was not due to what is popularly called a crisis of Indian character, or at least, not wholly due to it. This was in accordance with what human nature in a society always is where the process of modernization has been initiated by foreign or national rulers. Once the process has set in, it must be accelerated, though with due precautions. No attempt to reverse the process can succeed, though it can generate a lot of confusion and deflect the process for a while.

Similarly Gandhi's idea of secularism was totally impractical. Secularism, according to him, meant respect for all religions, for all religions essentially professed the same truth. Such a definition is purely visionary. For if one is a good Hindu, many of his religious practices are bound to be inconsistent with those of the Muslim or the Christian, particularly in case of the ordinary, non-intellectual people who are wholly emotionally involved in their religion. One cannot become tolerant of other religions by becoming more religious in his own creed.

What added to the sense of unreality created by this definition was Gandhi's own way of living, and the customs he followed in his public and private life. He lived like a Hindu saint, ate and drank like a Hindu saint and fasted like a Hindu saint. His speech was charged with the idioms of the Hindu religious-social reformer. Naturally, a number of history-conscious Muslims with modern education felt dissatisfied, and parted ways with the Congress. For Gandhi's secularism was basically medieval, not modern. The Emperor Akbar had tried to do and propagate the same thing. He tolerated a Hindu wife who worshipped her own gods in the emperor's fort. The modern meaning of secularism is based on total indifference to all religions and promotion of the scientific-rationalistic view of life. Not a state protection to all religions, but to leave all religions to themselves giving state patronage to none.

It is remarkable that no intellectual discussion, on these controversial aspects of Gandhian views, ever took place in those days. By the 1930s Gandhi had become an almost miraculous phenomenon, beyond the purview of intellect and reason. He was a modern Messiah in the land of Messiahs, to whom the people listened awe-struck and followed as though under a magic spell, rather than with understanding and conviction. The intellectuals of the country, belonging to all political parties, bowed before him in worshipful reverence. Those from foreign countries dashed to India to witness the miracle.

While this confusion prevailed among the non-governing political intellectuals, the number of intellectuals in the government and modern administration grew by leaps and bounds. In education the percentage had gone up to about 20% the colleges and universities were producing men and women with their interest awakened for imbibing more of modern knowledge. By the 1930s the British universities, particularly Oxford, Cambridge and London, had already become the Mecca of the academic Indian intellectuals. Even while the Gandhian movement took effect in boycotting foreign goods and foreign education, hundreds of Indian educated men were going to England for higher education and specialized training. When they returned they became the silent but pervasive means of creating a desire for a modern society with more widespread modern education and modern ways of living. Through them, and through the social and political benefits flowing from the British rule, emerged modern values, not professed but implicitly accepted. And, by and large, these people were essentially indifferent to Gandhi's programs, but even they professed support to them because they too wished for Independence.

Independence was made into an issue of over-riding and over-whelming importance, which drowned for the time being the historical contradictions inherent in the growth of Indian society.

PART 2

THE SITUATION TODAY

Chapter Seven

POST-INDEPENDENCE DISSIPATION

Political independence came to India, accompanied by the tragedy of its partition into two countries. The moment of rejoicing for the intellectual-political elite was also the moment of mourning for a large mass of agonized, insulted, angry, people who had been bereft of their near and dear ones and suffered untold miseries not of their making. To them partition came as a huge calamity. Nevertheless they bore the disaster by and large with exemplary fortitude,

Could partition have been prevented? The question is awkward and embarrassing in the extreme, particularly to those political personalities who were in some way or other involved in the tragic drama. Most of them have maintained absolute silence about the whole thing. Meanwhile, historians have been busy finding answers to the question. More often than not, their answers have been in terms of personalities rather than social forces in operation with their own irreversible compulsions.

One of such important but hitherto unidentified forces was Gandhi's style of functioning as a political leader, and his anti-modernistic and anti-intellectual attitude to problems facing the society. His socio-political attitude was almost wholly conditioned by his own personal spiritual problem, which itself was basically of the traditional Hindu nature. It may be true that Gandhi did not approve of the partition, and he did not rejoice over the independence of truncated India drenched red in the blood of communal riots. But that does not absolve him from the responsibility of having created, though completely unknowingly, a situation which gave rise to the demand for partition.

The problem of partition did not drop out of the blue. It was the culmination of the process that had registered its beginning with the Hindu-Muslim riots in 1921. The process could have been reversed soon after that, but for Gandhi's continued policy of making a medley of religion and politics, and his own methodology of fighting a political battle with religious weapons. There could be hardly any doubt that Gandh's Hindu appearance and upholding of Hindu values were instrumental in arousing the Hindu traditions of India. Gandhi's insistence in his preachings on the need for religious tolerance could not work alone. By the 1930s the Muslim intellectuals had become acutely conscious of their having been, not long ago, rulers from whom the Britishers had snatched power. In other words they had become power-hungry. Since the political struggle was limited to the manipulation of affairs by the intellectuals, alone without any effective participation of the masses, it was not unnatural nor unexpected that the Muslim intellectuals should stake their claim to adequate share in power if it was to be transferred to Gandhi's Congress party. Partition thus was the inescapable result of Gandhi's antiquarian political policies and economic programs, which no doubt produced miraculous results then, but showed the seeds of dissension between the two rival communities. This, coupled with the impatience of the intellectual-politicians to rule, precipitated the partition.

Whatever the reason, one thing was clear. Independence had been achieved by the intellectuals of the country, and it was their responsibility to preserve and strengthen it. The task was far from easy not only because of the multiplicity of problems bred by the partition, but also because of the Indian population lying inert for centuries, under the influence of their traditional primitive culture. To them freedom had come as an enigma and much too suddenly, and they were therefore baffled about what was expected of them to do. They stood and waited for orders from above, expecting the leaders to do whatever was to be done, since the latter had received independence on their own from the British. The masses had not fought for independence, and certainly not for partition. And therefore, they never really got involved in the gigantic work of social reconstruction. Consequently, this too became the sole responsibility of the intellectual-political leaders, both within the government as well as outside it.

In the circumstances Jawaharlal Nehru must be given full credit for trying to make a modern nation of the amorphous country that was transferred to his care at the time of independence. Fortunately, he also received in legacy an extremely well-trained, cool-headed, civil service, a well-trimmed army, an efficient police force, a judiciary of an excellent order, a whole system of modern uniform education throughout the country, a country-wide net-work of modern communication (radio, wireless telephone, teleprinter etc.) and transport (automobiles, trains, aeroplanes etc.) and numerous codes relating to the governance of the country. It was also a country where industrialization, on however modest a scale, had begun. Modern urban living had come to be looked upon by the common man and woman as desirable and worth aspiring for, despite whatever Gandhi preached. In fact, it would be found that more industrial undertakings were established in India in the 1930s than ever before. Consequently a large number of urban and semi-urban complexes grew up, and big cities were modernized. Such advantages as these had never before accrued to any new regime of government.

Undoubtedly Nehru tried to make full use of these advantages. Due to his sagacity and also forthrightness in this endeavour, he had a fair measure of success in tackling the immediate problems of refugee rehabilitation and the Kashmir dispute, each a gigantic task in itself. Then there was the mountainous task of providing sustenance to the teeming millions not to mention the equally urgent tasks of providing shelter, clothing, education and work for them.

What is relevant here is to note that in solving the problems, Nehru, true to his picture of an intellectual democrat, never sought ready-made solutions formulated and suitable to other countries. He always sought new ideas and new ways. When they were suggested to him or they occurred to him, he would try to implement them enthusiastically.

Secondly, he was a firm believer in the rational and scientific methods, and stood ultimately for the total modernization of all aspects of Indian life. He too, like many others, had sat at the feet of Gandhi, but he was never an orthodox Gandhian. He was surely a Gandhian in moral-ethical matters; but in matters of social and economic reconstruction he was a champion of modern scientific-technological methodology. In fact, he alone could go ahead with the plans of modernizing Indian agriculture, industry, commerce and social practices in the name of Gandhi, for it was well-known that he was Gandhi's chosen political heir.

Thirdly, Nehru was a confirmed democrat with an unshakable faith in the validity of individual liberty, with all the freedom that went with it. Even at the great risk of slow rate of economic growth, at a time when it was most urgently and immediately needed, he would abide by democratic norms. No prosperity at the cost of democracy seemed to be his motto. In fact, if he were forced to choose between the two, he would undoubtedly have chosen democracy rather than prosperity. Had he wanted, he could have declared himself a dictator and the whole country would have applauded. It would have been much easier for him to do this and perhaps, more necessary. But he was determined to train his people in the democratic mode of living, and through practice instill in them the virtues of it.

Nehru failed in many of his objectives; but where he succeeded immensely was in releasing and accelerating the complex processes of modernization of the entire society, and the entire social outlook. It is no longer possible to reverse this process without producing economic and social chaos. Nor is it possible even to modify it without causing a stagnation growth.

Nehru's failures, however, are more generic in nature than related to his personal failings. They are the failings of any intellectual politician placed in similar circumstances. Every intellectual is a visionary, and Nehru was a great visionary. His vision of India was different from Gandhi's anti-intellectual and pro-traditional vision of India. Nehru's vision encompassed the industrial richness of the science-technology, based on America and the intellectual achievement of modern Europe. The India of Nehru's dream was a mighty nation in all aspects of life.

In the enthusiasm of his visionary contemplation, he often lost touch with certain aspects of reality. More than many of his colleagues, he wished to believe that the masses of India had actually fought the battle of freedom with sufficient awareness of why and what they were fighting for. Since lakhs of people would always turn out to listen to him, he had perhaps reasons to believe so. He would never accept the fact that the actual situation was just the opposite, that people came to listen to him more out of curiosity to have a glimpse of the England-returned son of a fabulously rich father, of the one who was the closest to Bapu. He would therefore introduce mostly such plans and programs as required mass-participation for their success: the building of dams through voluntary labour; community development blocks; community projects and a host of others. Despite big financial and moral support from other democratic nations, all these schemes proved failures, for the basic assumptions underlying the idea were mistaken. The masses did not respond to the call in any considerable measure, except when they were paid for the work done. Gradually all the schemes meant to be based on voluntary mass-participation had to be somehow completed through government and official channels.

This happened because Nehru tended to think that as with the European people, the Indians would put in their best if offered adequate social and personal incentives in the task of nation-building. He did not take the cultural factor into account. He could not imagine that the masses, suddenly confronted with what was described to them as independence, did not know what to do. They expected their government to do everything for them. Basically, their attitude to the new national government was no different from their attitude to the old British government. Nothing had happened in their lives to warrant such a change of attitude. They had never fought nor participated voluntarily in the so-called struggle for freedom. The struggle had not touched them in any way to bring about a reorientation in their attitude. It had been waged in the cities. When the power was transferred to the Congress leaders, the masses watched as mere spectators, thinking all the time of themselves as the governed and never really dreaming that they were required to play a vital role in the making of the new government.

The one section of society which really was elated with a sense of triumph was that of the intellectuals. They alone understood fully the whole import of political freedom, for they had "fought" for it. Throughout the more militant period of the freedom struggle the leaders had inculcated into the minds of students, teachers, lawyers, journalists, bureaucrats and writers, that intellectual pursuits were really not very important or valuable. They were exhorted to leave their professions and pursuits, and join the freedom struggle, which a large number of them did. They went to jail, suffered and used their talents for the service of the nation. Some students gave up studies; teachers gave up teaching. Writers wrote poems and stories with stirring appeal to the youth to die for freedom. Some certainly became martyrs, but all those who lived on hoped secretly that they would one day be amply rewarded and prayed for the arrival of that day while they were yet alive. When freedom came, the mantle of power fell on them. They became now the rulers. Overnight, college lecturers became high ranking executive officers in the newly constituted Indian Administrative Service. Many of the old foreign service personnel were retained, and hasty recruitments were made to fill in other posts fallen vacant. Intellectual politicians became ministers and governors and speakers and chairmen of scores of commissions. The intellectuals' dream had come true. They were now governing their own country.

On the face of it, there was nothing wrong in this elevation of the intellectuals to the executive and administrative positions. In fact, this was inevitable in the circumstances, and also certainly desirable. Indeed, for about a decade after freedom, the intellectuals seemed to fit admirably well into their new roles. Then began the dissipation.

It was apparent after about a decade that the established system could not accommodate all intellectual politicians of the pre-independence days. Many of those who were kept out of power now turned into agitators, and started using the same strategies which they as well as those in power had used against foreign rule. They incited the students, persuaded the teachers, coaxed the journalists and stirred the masses to serve their own ends. But the unity in this agitation was no longer possible. Every group of people joined the agitation for its own specific ends different from this other. The common goal was a substantial share in this power to govern, and thereby enjoy unearned privileges and unearned income, which those in power had enjoyed for a decade. This gave rise to a general desire for quick and easy gains, which from the intellectuals seeped down to the non-intellectuals and the common man. The way to easy and quick gains, it had become clear in a decade, was not through the rigours of intellectual pursuits, but through becoming leaders of paltry causes.

Consequently, the entire intellectual atmosphere of the country was thoroughly debased. The attainment of excellence in intellectual pursuits, which comes from years of hard work done with single-minded devotion to it, no longer remained the real objective before the intellectuals, though they continued to profess it. To attain state recognition with a view to winning positions of authority and power became their chief aim. The only seal of excellence which came to be recognized as of any worth was that of state recognition, in the form of awards or the offer of lucrative posts. Soon there was a race for these posts, which included intellectuals of all sorts without any rules of etiquette or conduct.

The clamour for participating in this race became noisier when the various Akademies were established, with the high objectives of creating and maintaining standards of excellences in the various arts. Behind this was perhaps Nehru's dream of creating something equivalent to the Academies in European countries. Owing to the socio-political circumstances from which the intellectuals had emerged in India, the Akademies, far from trying to achieve the high objectives set before them, turned out to be instruments of lowering the standard, including the potential excellence. This would be immediately evident to any one who cares to compare the quality of Indian intellectual attainments in the arts sciences and literature, before the establishment of the Akademies, with their achievements after they came into being.

As for the bureaucratic elite, nothing indeed had changed substantially with the coming of independence and the departure of the British. The old foreign bosses had been replaced by new national bosses, whom they could handle more easily for their own gain. With precious few exceptions, the new bosses, ministers, deputy ministers and others, had no idea of the work they were required to do, particularly when the whole style of working was exactly the same as during the British rule. Naturally, the new bosses came to depend upon the bureaucrats much more heavily than ever before, nay, almost entirely. Soon after the initial apprehension and sense of uncertainty at the the time of independence, the bureaucratic elite soon emerged with greater self-assurance and confidence in its own power than ever before.

The total result of all this was the continued alienation of the entire intellectual class from the masses. The irony of the situation was that the masses had remained politically unconcerned through the freedom struggle and were now gullible enough to play readily into the hands of the intellectuals. All intellectuals in all their activities, though based upon borrowed concepts, swore by the masses, and promised them miracles in most high-sounding terms.

The situation started worsening further with the failures or, at best, the partial successes of the five-year plans. The governing intellectuals had to cover up the near-failures of the economic plans in high-sounding words, so that they might appear as near-successes. On the other hand, the non-governing intellectuals had to become the new saviours of the people still rotting in poverty and ignorance. They were the new revolutionaries bred and brought up on foreign books, foreign theories and news of foreign experiments with revolutionary methods. They were quite convinced that since one generation of the intellectuals had won freedom and become corrupt with power, it was the responsibility of the next generation of intellectuals to undertake the task of social reconstruction on certain revolutionary principles.

Thus both the governing and the non-governing intellectuals contributed to the creation of an unreal situation, in which the whole promise of the pre-independence days seemed to be dissolving. With the view of the future blocked, it is only natural that the intellectuals should have found the paper and the platform as the safest spots to tread on. To exhibit their abilities from these two spots to the masses became their chief, in fact, sole concern. Thus it was that the paper-work came to be a substitute for real work. Nay, it became even better than a mere substitute. Paper figures, data, statistics, charts, graphs, all enigmatic and so appearing highly impressive to the masses, came to dominate the newspapers, magazines, government handouts, reports and also lectures, seminars and symposia. Where paper-work is backed by solid real work, statistical figures and charts are a virtue. But where paper-work is not backed by solid real work, they become a mere a cover-up for the ugly reality.

Since the majority of intellectuals now were the rulers, or aspiring to become rulers or lackeys of the rulers, they had to impress the few other apparently opposition leaders as also the masses. They soon become experts in the art of evading real work and surprising with mere paper work. It spread soon from the government offices to the semi-government and non-government offices, and, finally to the universities, colleges and schools throughout the country. Thus a total hollowness came to prevail underneath the appearance of intense intellectual activities.

Chapter Eight

ROUND AND ROUND THE PRICKLY-PEAR

The rise and fall of what we call the progressive intellectuals in India during the sixties and early seventies has been a phenomena of great sociological curiosity. They came with so much of froths in their mouths, frowns on their foreheads. For a while they fumed and fretted, paraded the streets, shouted something undecipherable from the platforms and hatched juvenile conspiracies in the dark, then they almost vanished into thin air. For they were nothing more than insubstantial projections of the intellectual ideas and idealisms propagated and practised vigorously abroad.

In many ways Jawaharlal Nehru was responsible for both their growth and disintegration. His own life-style and style of functioning in the government soon after independence began to betray a predilection for aristocracy, pomp and exhibitionism. His defence of the grandeur of imperial times bred disaffection and dissatisfaction among the educated youth, deriving particularly from both the lower and upper sections of the middle class. Most of them were still imbued with the idealism which Gandhi and Nehru in his pre-independence days used to preach to the nation. The youths were impatient for visible and concrete changes. But nothing seemed to change substantially. Governors with huge mansions and huge expanse of compounds, and the President with his monumental architectural complex, and perhaps the largest area of estate available to any head of a country anywhere in the world, were redolent more of the foreign imperial government than of the national democratic government. Economically these institutions were a useless liability, but Nehru defended them on the peculiar ground of the prestige of the nation, as though prestige were a matter of facade grandeur. But unconsciously this sense of false prestige came to dominate the mood of the nation. Perhaps if the plans had been full successes and the economic condition of the people ameliorated in some concrete form, maintenance of these institutions would not have bred dissatisfaction among the youth. While economically the country came to be wholly dependent on foreign aid, the expensive institutions of the erstwhile imperial age were allowed to continue on flimsy grounds.

Because of Nehru's own emotional and intellectual attachment to the West, he showed his preference for foreign things, and foreign trained personnel and so on. This, and the widespread awareness of the superiority of western goods led to the retention of western values. Soon the foreign returned became the ideal image: a foreign degree, even a foreign visit, served as a sure passport to social prestige and well-paid jobs in both government and private offices. The country thus came to be infested with intellectuals bred and brought up in foreign fashion, on foreign thought. They talked glibly in abstract language learnt by rote from books by foreign experts or foreign-returned scholars, and hated to see reality outside the seminar rooms and conference halls.

The progressive intellectuals arose apparently in reaction to the above two factors. They professed to belong to the soil of Indian society, and promised to the masses that if they came to power they would eradicate poverty in the twinkle of an eye. They aimed to overhaul the entire political, social and economic system once they came to power.

Yet essentially these progressive intellectuals too were not different from the other group of liberal, democratic intellectuals. Like the latter, the former too were not the product of the soil and had grown from theoretical acquaintances with the history of revolutions in the USSR and China and a sentimental infatuation with the revolutionary heroes of those countries. Since the idea of revolution had been derived from other countries, soon the progressive intellectuals began to live on certain cults of imitative appearance and demeanour. Since they were reluctant to go to the masses and involve them in mass actions, except on rare occasions for demonstrations, these new intellectuals chose to concentrate on the colleges and universities, tea-corners and coffee houses of the big cities from where according to them the revolution in India was destined to begin.

Thus in the ultimate analysis these progressive intellectuals were more derivative, pretentious, and alienated from the reality of the social situation, than the liberal intellectuals. But for some time they dominated the Indian intellectual scene. They wore crumpled, coarse and dirty trousers and *kurta* with a long-striped shoulder-bag stuffed with pamphlets and periodicals, grew long and matted hair, sometimes ill-kept beards and moustaches and put on tattered chappals. They enjoyed discussions and theories of revolution over cups of coffee or tea or mugs of beer, and argued passionately and loudly. Often they flexed their muscles in support of their knowledge of theories. For though they were all progressive, they were divided into several sects of progressiveness. Marx, of course, all of them swore by, but each sect claimed to know more about what Marx had written or implied than the other. Each sect obviously was founded upon a particular Marxist hero, from Lenin and Stalin down to Mao, Minh, and Che Guevera. The influence and power of the contestants was proved by their ability to quote from their intellectual-revolutionary heroes and, above all, in their capacity for coining militant slogans.

These slogans were then besmeared in red of varying intensity on the walls of the university and college buildings, not unoften on the roads and footpaths too. Again these slogans constituted the main subjects of the small revolutionary "journals" which mushroomed all over the four big city-centres of revolution.

Quite a few of these militant revolutionaries derived from families of rich feudal or business or high government officials. Bringing out such a "journal" of four to sixteen or forty pages was an easy pastime, but which gave them the rare satisfaction of being known as intellectuals.

In retrospect, it is quite clear that this spurt of the fashionable Marxist intellectuals was to a large extent the result of imitating the New Left movement in France, Britain and America. Like their masters in the west,[1] they preached "revolution" in

[1] George Watsan, "Was the New Left a Success !" *Encounter*, October 1975.

highly intellectual language, to serve their own ends of securing positions in government and semi-government offices, universities, or to ensure promotions to higher cadres. Quite a few of these self-styled Marxist intellectuals succeeded immensely in their objectives here in India too.

In India left-adventurism often has taken dangerous turns, such as in Telangana and later in the Naxalite uprisings. Both of them were caused by dreamers of revolution, rather than a band of well-trained revolutionaries with a keen sense of Indian social reality. Since the killing of men in authority who belonged to the upper privileged exploiting class in other countries had generated a revolution, it would, they thought, succeed also in India. Telengana was specifically related to the vast mass of peasantry exploited by the zamindars and landlords, and was rather spontaneous in its outburst. The Naxalbari uprising on the other hand was the result of putting into practice well-devised programs based on a borrowed philosophy of revolution. Of the two, the Naxalbari uprising was seemingly more intellectual in character, and therefore enlisted in its cadre a larger number of educated people, particularly students and college and university teachers. It did not only offer intellectual excitement to the educated youths bored with routine dull teaching and stereotyped education system. It also offered them the thrill of violent murder and adventurous escape, a kind of life to which they felt so irresistibly drawn.

Both the uprisings failed ratner ingloriously. These quixotic intellectual tales could not have had any other kind of ending. Whatever other causes of the failure of these uprisings, one is quite evident for any one to see. The general Indian people, howsoever poor, are totally averse to solving their problems through mass killings. Not because they are morally averse to killing human beings, because in communal riots they kill each other brutally with the least of compunctions. Yet they believe that the problem of poverty cannot be solved by human effort or governmental action, let alone by killing the rich whom God has rewarded for their virtuous deeds in the previous life. The task of educating such a mass of people in Marxism and preparing them for revolution would baffle even a handful of Maos. The Indian people believe in *dan*, charity, which partly explains why Vinoba's *bhoodan* movement caught up so easily in

Telengana itself and, later, in the entire country.

Right adventurism too, made its advent on the Indian scene, with the success of Vinoba in apparently extinguishing the smouldering fire in Telengana. It lured away potentially brilliant intellectuals from healthy social-intellectual activities. For Vinoba's movement has been basically anti-intellectual and anti-modern life, as was Gandhi's during the pre-independence days. But while Gandhi's anti-intellectual devices served well as an instrument of arousing the masses who, at that time, would not have responded to intellectual appeal, Vinoba's movement has only tended to create confusion about the process of modernization introduced by the government agencies. If Vinoba succeeded in weaning people away from violence, he also weaned them away from seeking solutions to problems in the modern intellectual way. A large number of socialist intellectuals led by Jayprakash Narain fell in the trap laid by Vinoba, not to mention other intellectuals from various political parties, educational institutions and other sections of the society.

Right-adventurism assumed many forms and took in fact a heavier toll of Indian intellectuals than left adventurism. For one thing, it was socially respectable, and venerable because it was in accord with the traditional Hindu way of life. The Shri Aurobindo Ashram at Pondicherry claimed the largest number of highly-placed intellectuals such as university professors, high-court judges, eminent lawyers, scientists, writers, bureaucrats and converted them to anti-intellectual faith in the power and the glory of supra-intellectual consciousness.

Soon other yogis and maharishis mushroomed, promising the bliss of life through sex, meditation, yoga, prayer, tantra etc. It is a notable fact that these new cults of right-adventurism could not attract the masses in large number, but they did readily attract the intellectuals. The reason behind this was the deep anti-intellectual drive inherent in the Hindu culture. Even in the highly educated and highly modernized Indian, there is a furtive but insistent urge to subscribe to traditional beliefs and ways of life. They were moved to this more readily because the westerners by joining these anti-intellectual cults had lent them respectability and sanction.

Both these extremes of reaction in the two opposite directions made Jawaharlal Nehru's task of modernizing Indian social, cultural and intellectual life more difficult. His solutions, though offered with the best of intentions, only confounded the already confused intellectual situation and impeded the growth of free inquiry, and the acquisition of knowledge.

In the first place Nehru tried to incorporate in his economic plans and political programs almost all shades of progressive thought : socialist, communist, democratic, scientific. This produced one desirable effect, in as much as he took the wind out of the sails of the left opposition parties. Since they too had no roots in the masses, they tended to grow vociferous but stagnant and uncertain of themselves. Nehru's foreign policy of non-alignment with any bloc and friendship with countries of the opposite camps strengthened his national image, of being the most progressive of all progressives. This nevertheless created a confusion in the Indian intellectual world, tended to blunt the outlines of distinction and categories and classifications of the thought-process. Inevitably it promoted a tendency, which soon became widespread, to play upon and with words with a view to confuse the sense behind the facade.

Secondly, Nehru adopted a policy of inducting the unattached intellectuals into the government offices, at all levels from the highest to the lowest. Apparently this served three purposes. One, the government obtained the services of the best brains available in the country. Two, the entry of the eminent intellectuals in the government offices enhanced the prestige of those offices. Three, the intellectuals too felt gratified with the prestige and power these offices brought to them, and for the sake of these gains they did not mind remaining content and silent, beconing vociferous yes-men of all government policies and helpless spectators of government actions, even when they did not personally approve of them. A typical example of this was Dr Rajendra Prasad as the President of India. As President he had no option, generally speaking, but to put his seal of approval on all policies of Nehru. When he ceased to be President after the completion of his second term, he revealed that he was personally against Nehru's policy of conceding the Chinese claim on Tibet.

In the long-run interest of intellectual growth in the country, the policy of harnessing the intellectuals into government offices for nation-building work did more harm than good. If these intellectuals—particularly those academically-inclined such as Dr Sarvapalli Radhakrishnan, Dr Zakir Hussain, and a host of others, had been left to their intellectual preoccupations, they would have most probably contributed more substantially to the intellectual growth of the nation. They would have been free then, to produce original ideas in their respective disciplines, provide objective criticism of the government policies and programs, and thereby, promote free and fearless thinking in the country.

Secondly, the policy induced a strong inclination in the intellectuals to seek government offices and regard these offices as the highest rewards. At lower levels, this created a situation in which intellectual work for the sake of enriching world ideas came to be looked upon as a fool's pursuit. The wise intellectuals started devising ways and means of getting somehow into the government offices. Soon the intellectuals of the country vied with each other to grab the coveted offices by all sorts of means, fair or foul, in fact, more foul than fair, which included bribery, appeasement, coercion, concession etc. depending upon the need of the hour.

The promotion to higher ranks was no longer, determined by the work done and recognition won in the national and international community of intellectuals. It went, as Iago says ironically to Othello, by preferment, personal whim and strong self-interest. Lecturers in the colleges clamoured to become professors in the universities, professors manipulated to become vice-chancellors and vice-chancellors ministers. Writers were not satisfied with writing and yearned to join departments of government publication, or administrative offices in the AIR. Men of the judiciary waited patiently to be tipped for the chairmanship of various commissions. Newspaper correspondents and editors enjoyed becoming ambassadors. Even scientists concerned themselves more with being included in government sponsored delegations, and with obtaining high posts in government agencies than with the laboratory work they were required to do.

It may be argued that in all countries of the world intellectuals are induced to join government offices, and quite a number of them do so. Yet in no other country do the intellectuals come to regard these offices as the be-all and end-all of their existence. This is peculiar to India. The moment the intellectual obtains this office, he stops his intellectual work and devotes all his time to administrative work, partly because it is unavoidable, but mostly because he likes it infinitely more than any intellectual preoccupation. If it were not so, there would have been cases of intellectuals getting disgusted with office-jobs and resigning in order to resume their intellectual pursuits. With one or two exceptions, such cases in India have never occurred. On the contrary there are instances galore of intellectuals indulging in mutual bickering and back-biting, to obtain the offices, and to try to maintain them at all cost.

It is doubtful if the squabbles of Indian intellectuals for government offices can be wholly attributed to their living in the intellectual provinces and aspiring to belong to the metropolis, as Edward Shils says.[2] More convincing would appear to be two other factors, the one historical and the other cultural. Historically, since intellectuals had fought for freedom and obtained it, they came to regard themselves as legitimate heirs to the departed rulers and were impatient to act as rulers in whatever limited capacity they could. Culturally, they were averse to and had no real faith in the efficacy or utility of intellectual work. Abstract philosophical speculation or mechanical chanting of the *mantras* for the salvation of the soul is a different matter altogether. But work which is related to aspects of social living is not something which the Indian mind is culturally prone to accept. The traditional Indian concept of a happy life is one without work put replete with all the pleasures of the senses. The Indian intellectuals, more than the Indian masses, are subject to these historical and cultural factors, for they are the true inheritors of both history and culture.

Modern liberal scientific education has not changed their fundamental outlook and behaviour to any remarkable degree. It has enriched their mind, but failed to modify their basic attitude to life. The hold of Hindu culture on the Indian mind has been so strong and deep that liberal modern education, with its appeal to the intellect and reason, has itself been wholly trivialized. Far from adapting their traditional life to the

---

[2]Shils. "Metropolis and Province in the Intellectual Community," *Changing India*. Asia, Bombay, 1961.

demands of modern life, the Hindus have adapted modernity to their own traditional mould. What Robert Sinai says about the failure of industrialization to modernize Hindu society and the success of the latter in "hinduising the industrial and modern elements...and distorting, corrupting and devitalizing them in the process" could also be said about the traditional cultural attitude vis-a-vis modern education.[3]

This process of adaptation has bred a peculiar brand of Indian intellectuals, who are neither truly traditional nor modern, but both superficially. They are not torn between the old and the new as M.N. Srinivas,[4] would have us believe. An awareness of these contradictions usually leads to creativity in ideas and literature. The Indian intellectuals suffer from no such sense of contradictions. They are at peace with themselves because intellectual conflicts and contradictions do not affect the depth of their being.

The inevitable result of all this is the creation of a paradoxical state, in which the intellectuals appear to keep busy without producing anything worthwhile, mouthing words without meaning and moving without progress.

---

[3] Sinai, "Modernization and the Poverty of the Social Sciences," *Modernization of Underdeveloped Societies*, A. R. R. Desai, ed., Thacker and Co., Bombay, 1971.

[4] Srinivas, "Modernization : A Few Queries" in *ibid*.

Chapter Nine

THE LANGUAGE TANGLE

Language is the chief tool of the intellectual. It is not a mere medium of expression. It is also a means of understanding the world around. Perception is not enough, at least for the purpose of intellectual activities. Language helps clarify, categorize and, at the same time, synthesize the perceived elements into new wholes. It modifies perception itself.

Apart from language, there are other tools of expression used by artists. The painter has colour for his tool, and the musician has sound. As for the sculptor, the space itself is his medium of apprehending as well as expressing the world. The same could be said about the dancer, except that his perception of the space is always related to movement.

The painter, the musician, the sculptor and the dancer are, however, artists who work in the realm beyond language or, better still, prior to language. Primarily their mode of perception as well as expression is emotional and not intellectual. If and when the intellectual element is there, it is subservient to the nature of the prevailing central emotion.

For other intellectuals which include scientists, literary writers, social thinkers, economists, politicians, teachers, lawyers, philosophers, teachers and journalists, the language remains the chief tool of analysis and communication of ideas. Among these, the mathematicians and natural scientists make the least use of language as such. They depend more upon the use of figures, symbols and equations than upon words, for the communication of their ideas and meaning. Nevertheless, even in their case, a certain kind of proficiency in the language they use helps in acquiring precision and exactitude in expression.

For the other intellectuals, however, an adequate proficiency in the language they use is an indispensable pre-condition for their activities. The worth of their ideas is invariably linked up with the way they handle language. Great historians, great philosophers, great social thinkers, in fact, great intellectuals in any field, have been great masters of language—each one with a distinct style, distinct idiom and distinct nuance. Marx could not have written his *Das Kapital* in the style of Calvin; nor would have Sartre found it possible to write in the style of Marx. The theme invents its own idiom and style, not only in poetry and drama and novel, but also in social literature

The purpose of the above analysis is to bring home the axiomatic truth that there is a very deep relationship between originality of thought and proficiency in the language, used with all its nuances. It is in this context that the language problem must be seen in India. If the production of original ideas about man and his society is the ultimate goal, the choice of language is of uppermost importance. In fact, there is no alternative to the choice of writing in one's own language.

There is the rub. In nations which are leaders of today's intellectual world, the problem of language does not exist. The language of the writer is the language of the whole society, intellectual or non-intellectual. The proficiency he has gained is as much natural as acquired. In India however, the situation is much more complex.

History has installed English as the language of intellectual activities in India. To say that it is the unfortunate consequence of about a hundred and fifty years of British rule is to ignore half the truth. For supposing there had been no British domination of India, in all likelihood there would have been today no Indian intellectual. Most probably India would have remained divided into many sovereign states and many languages, with Urdu establishing itself as a language of inter-state communication. Since education would have continued in its primitive mode and confined to the memorizing of the sacrosanct scriptures, the possibility of free intellectual inquiry would never have arisen. It is in this sense at least that the British rule was fortunate, for the future intellectual development in India. The British rule initiated the two processes of modernization and intellectualization, which must always inevitably go together, on such a firm footing as to make it impossible to check their growth.

Through the British Raj came English to India, and through English came the urge of modernization and intellectualization of the Indian society. During the period of the freedom struggle, this aspect of the Raj had to be played down for tactical reasons. Anything related to the British had to be condemned to arouse nationalist sentiments. So English was often described as the language of the imperialist, though the irony of the leaders themselves being highly trained in English went unnoticed in the enthusiasm of those days. Hindi offered itself naturally as the alternative to the language of domination, and people of different regions seemed voluntarily to have agreed on this. Even C. Rajgopalachari is known to have vigorously espoused the cause of disseminating and developing Hindi. Apart from the fact that Hindi was found to be the most widely spoken language in India, it was also patronised by Gandhi who popularized it in the non-Hindi speaking regions through his journals and prayer meetings. In those days anything which served to arouse national pride and had the blessing of Gandhi was accepted without dispute or debate.

With the attainment of freedom however, the situation changed radically; and more so, after Gandhi's death. With Nehru's strong preference for the modernization of the Indian society, English and the English liberal education were retained as before, even made more intensified and wide-spread. Although it was not listed as one of the Indian languages in the Indian Constitution, it continued to be, anomalous as it may sound, the language of the Parliamentary, legal, and legislative activities. The authorized version of the Constitution continued to be in a language which it itself did not recognize to be Indian. Thereafter, the authorized version of all bills, acts, judgements, awards, reports, circulars at all levels, central, state and district, continued to be the original English version. The language of good schools, of colleges and universities also continued to be English. As for business and commerce, English was the only language to be used. Whatever its official position, English continued to be the language of the people who really matter : rulers, policy-and-decision makers, better-educated, cultured, intelligent persons, big businessmen, fabulously paid executives, sales-men, journalists, bureaucrats, and so on and so forth.

The reaction was bound to occur, and it occurred soon. The advocates of Hindi raised slogans, held noisy protest meetings, incited the Hindi-speaking people to anger and fury, and thus succeeded in creating a near-riot situation in the country. They swore by the Constitution, by the Father of the Nation, by the numerical strength of the Hindi-speaking people, and claimed to be the genuine patriots.

For Jawaharlal Nehru an extremely confusing situation was created. He was definitely not against Hindi, or Hindustani, as he preferred to call it. Yet he knew that the socio-economic goal he had set for the country would not be served by adopting Hindi as it was. The Hindi language and traditional Hindi culture, culture being inseparable from the language, would not serve the cause of modernization which required a scientific, liberal and humanistic approach. With Nehru this was of greater significance than the problem of retaining national unity. The latter was of course important, but Nehru's initial attitude to the English-Hindi problem is determined more by the former. National unity was not much of a problem for him even if he had overnight replaced English by Hindi even till as late as, say 1954. He had the Constitution in his favour, and, more than that, his own unchallenged and unchallengable leadership. In this respect, he enjoyed the sanction and authority of Gandhi as well. He could easily have done it, but he knew that the cultural-literary state in which Hindi was would certainly impede the process of modernization.

After 1954-1955, Hindi fanatics raised their angry fists and the non-Hindi people shuddered in fear of the language domination, which, in effect, meant power domination. The question of national unity became a more important consideration than pushing the pace of modernization. It was from then onward that Nehru had to deal delicately with the language problem, sometimes patronizing Hindi and pleading for it, sometimes patronizing English and pleading for it, conceding a point here to the one, and conceding another point there to the other. In pacifying both he always raised the question of national unity which had the virtue of silencing both the camps, at least for a while.

Thus language, which is primarily a medium of communication of thought, feeling and idea, and grows in accordance with the socio-economic and intellectual growth of the society, became a political issue after 1956-1957. This culminated in the language riots both in the northern and southern India in the '60's. Far from becoming a tool in the hands of the intellectuals, it became a tool in the hands of the power-seeking politicians. Since then the language problem has aroused much muddle-headed discussion, hardly ever based upon the facts and almost always clouded by chauvinistic fury.

For example, there are advocates of English in India, such as Professor C.D. Narsimhaia, who claim that the standard of excellence achieved in what has now come to be called Indo-Anglian literature is comparable to that of English literature produced in England. This fantastic claim is countered by another group of advocates of English, though orthodox English, led by Khushwant Singh and Dom Moraes who believe that Indo-Anglian literature even at its best is only a very mediocre and negligible achievement.

The case of creative literature, of the novel, poetry, drama, and the essay, stands apart. There can be no valid reasons for the continuation of writing creative literature in English, except by those who have gained sufficient aptitude in no other language than English and have an irresistible urge to write. There can be no legislation banning or permitting the writing of Indo-Anglian literature. So long as there will be a demand in the readers' market for Indo-Anglian literature, and there are writers to write and publishers to supply it, it will continue to be written. It is not related to the problem of language as a tool of the intellectual.

What is at issue here is the place and status of a language in the entire social set-up. This is not determined by creative literature. On the contrary, the latter is determined by the former. Indo-Anglian literature itself is the product of a hundred-year monopoly enjoyed by English in Indian society under the British rule. Its continuation has been made possible by English enjoying still complete supremacy over other Indian languages, as effective for all kinds of non-literary activities. (Not often, in the history of world literature, the excellence of literary achievements has been decisively conditioned by the excellence of achievement in non-literary literature of ideas and thought.)

It needs to be recalled that when Raja Ram Mohan Roy

made an impassioned appeal to the British Government, to introduce English as a medium of instruction in the Indian educational system, he never meant it to be used ever as a language of creative literature. In fact, he advocated for writing creative literature in Bengali. He himself wrote many of his reformist tracts in Bengali. As a result of this, English education was widely disseminated in Bengal, but also Bengali literature came to be written more profusely. In fact, the best achievements in Bengali literature were reached during the days when English was most widespread.

Raja Rammohan Roy pleaded for English because he had the sagacity to see that India would never come to realise its own glory, and make its own way in the future, without the liberal-scientific education which was possible only through English. This was a vital aspect of his reform of the superstitious and caste-ridden Hindu society. He aimed at killing two birds with one stone: divesting the orthodox brahmin pundits of their exclusive position in the society as a Sanskrit-knowing intellectual caste ; and, letting western liberal knowledge seep through English to all Indians, irrespective of caste and community.

Thus his plea for English was a plea for modernizing the Indian society, and for a vigorous intellectual life. There is no doubt that English served these two purposes as well as it could do on alien land. Even today English continues to serve these purposes, with more and more of the people's support.

Consider these facts for example. Even thirty years after Independence, despite official anti-English position and widespread anti-English feelings and prejudices, English continues to be the language of all official deliberations and communications. More books are published in English than in any other Indian regional language, or than perhaps books in all the regional languages put together. Our best national newspapers and journals are in English, with circulation figures which far exceed those of any other newspapers and journals in the regional languages. English still is the language of the B.A. & B.Sc. Honours and post-graduate studies, as well as of higher research in social as well as the natural sciences.

In addition, English continues to be the language of business and commerce. Almost all big business houses in the country, irrespective of the regions where they are situated, continue to transact their work in English. In fact it has come to acquire such a prestige in the entire business and commercial world that even small and petty traders are lured to use English on their sign-boards, and in their advertisement pieces. The amount of social prestige it enjoys can be imagined from the fact that many eminent anti-English agitators have wisely chosen to send their children to English medium schools in order that their prospects of employment and intellectual attainment are not marred. For whether it is a high ranking government job or a private job, the knowledge of English is an essential qualification.

The depths to which English has permeated into the Indian's intellectual, social, economic and cultural life would not have been possible, if, as is sometimes made out, English had been introduced in the beginning merely to train the Indians to serve as clerks. From the very beginning, English at a higher level of education served as a chief instrument of cultural, intellectual, and consequently political, reawakening in India. Paradoxically English, which Macaulay introduced with a view to anglicising the Indians and thereby turning them into staunch supporters of the British Raj, played an instrumental role in producing anti-Raj leaders in a large number who ultimately toppled the government. They did not topple English, for they know what they and the nation owed to English.

We tend to forget or ignore this background of English when we come to discuss its role in India today. We easily get into a state of chauvinistic fervour and forget to reason.

English today has come to establish itself as much more than a 'link language'. It is the language of higher intellectual activities. It is also the language of fashion, culture, sophistication, prestige and so on. There are many non-intellectual glamour journals of film and fashion, which use English as their medium. What is important to note is that in the sphere of higher intellectual activities English is the only language used. None of the other Indian languages including Hindi, is ever used for higher intellectual purposes. It seems that the regional Indian languages, including Hindi, have tacitly left the entire field of intellectual work to English and have limited themselves to non-intellectual, mainly literary, writings.

This should be clear to any one who takes a careful look at book publishing in India. While nearly 99 per cent of books published in English belong to subjects of intellectual interest such as social and natural sciences, current politics, culture, art and religion, 99 per cent of books published in other Indian languages including Hindi belong to fiction and poetry and rarely, drama. By definition fiction and poetry belong to the intellectual category, but, unfortunately, Indian fiction and poetry have very little intellectual content, almost nothing. One reason why the Indian regional literatures are so poor in drama, essays, memoirs, criticism, satire etc. is that these forms require a lively play of the intellect, which is not an important ingredient of the Indian creative writer.

Normally Hindi by now should have produced a handful of books of ideas and thought dealing with such problems as partition, economic planning, current political events, international diplomacy, sociological studies of Indian society and so on. While in English books by Indian authors on such and other allied subjects abound, there is *not a single* book available in Hindi, which is officially India's national language. In pursuance of the official policy, millions of rupees have been and are even now being spent on glossaries and dictionaries and directories of all kinds in Hindi by the various official bodies; but so far all efforts have been in vain. Hindi continues to be totally barren of the literature of ideas, owing to which it continues to churn out only third-rate and imitative creative literature, inferior to that of even some other Indian languages such as Bengali, Tamil and Marathi.

The same pattern stands out more clearly in the realm of journalism. There is not a single Hindi newspaper in the country which can compete with English newspapers, in respect of quality or circulation. Among periodicals, Hindi ones are the cheapest in taste and poorest in intellectual content. In English intellectual journals such as the *Economic and Political Weekly*, *Eastern Economist, Link, Mainstream, Quest, Swarajya* and a host of others, not to mention the numerous specialized journals of councils and institutes abound. Hindi cannot boast of having a single journal of this kind.

It is thus clear beyond dispute that Hindi, as an effection language of communication, has missed the bus altogether. The educated and the intellectual have not accepted it, which is only another way of saying that it has not developed in consonance with the needs of the time. It will continue to be politically exploited, but is not likely to become an adequate medium of intellectual activities in the fast changing social and economic situation.

English will, therefore, continue to be used in India by its intellectuals as medium of expression. As a medium of apprehending the world it may never be, since it is hardly the mother-tongue of any community in India, excepting for a few Anglo-Indian families. If it has been accepted as the official state language in Meghalaya, it is not because it is the mother-tongue of the Nagas. It is because they have no written language of their own, and their mother-tongue is wholly oral and extremely primitive in character.

As the tool of the intellectual in India, since it is almost no one's mother-tongue, English is bound to be an imperfect tool; adequate as a medium of expression, but inadequate as a medium of apprehending the social reality. Yet even with this limitation, English alone is now destined to continue as the language of the educated, intelligent, cultured, thinking, inquiring, modernized Indian people.

Yet there is a snag here. If English has to continue, as it will in India, it has to be made completely an Indian language. At present since it is taken as a foreign language, its standard of excellence is set in America and Britain; and Indian intellectuals try to imitate it. As a result of this, they would like to earn recognition from the intellectuals of those countries. For that in turn ensures recognition from intellectuals in this country. If a book by an Indian author is taken note of in Britain and America, it catches the attention of the reading public here too.

As a result of this, a peculiar situation has arisen in the Indian intellectual world. Almost invariably, significant intellectual work done in India first gets into publication in the British or American journals; and then it travels back to this country after a couple of years or so. This certainly harms the nation's intellectual growth in various ways. In the first place, this deprives the nation of its own intellectuals. Secondly, with the craving to be published in Britain and America, more often than not, Indian intellectuals work on projects which are of little or no relevance to the problems facing their country today. Thirdly, having won foreign laurels, and specialized in subjects more immediately suited to western society, these intellectuals feel alienated in their own country. Most of them try to migrate to the West, but only a handful of them succeed. Those who have to stay on here continue to feel unsettled and unwilling to put their best into their work.

The language problem, of course, is not the only reason behind this sorry state of affairs. Scores of socio-politico-economic factors are responsible for this stalemate in the Indian intellectual life. Nevertheless, language most certainly is one of the most important factors. The Indian intellectuals write with an inhibiting amount of language-consciousness, always consciously or unconsciously imitating their western masters both in respect of style and ideas. Had there been a distinctly Indian English with its own character, vocabulary, idiom, nuances and standard of excellence, commonly accepted throughout India, the intellectuals of this country would never have hankered after western patronage and occupied themselves more freely with the production of original ideas.

What is required is what has happened in Australia, Canada and even America. English as written and spoken in Australia has an identity of its own, which is distinct from Canadian and American English. Similarly English has to evolve in India in a manner that it develops into a distinctly Indian language, with an independent intellectual life of its own.

Whether it will ever happen will depend upon the calibre of the Indian intellectuals, and the originality of their ideas relevant to the modernization of society. Originality of Indian thought is generally misconstrued to be related merely to India's past, to its culture and philosophy. While that too is extremely necessary, the originality in thought required can emerge only from totally imbibing the available modern knowledge and planning the future with this basis.

Only then the vision of Raja Rammohan Roy and Jawaharlal Nehru will become a reality. This is a challenge for the Indian intellectuals. At present however, they do not even seem to be fully aware of the challenge.

Chapter Ten

EDUCATIONAL AND CULTURAL DOLDRUMS

Higher educational and cultural institutions such as colleges, universities, research centres, cultural academies etc. are the nursery of the intellectual. It is there that the seeds of his future accomplishments and achievements are sown in him and also begin to sprout. The fruits come later when he has completed his formal education and come to grapple with living problems.

In this process of the growth of the intellectual, the role of the lower educational institutions too cannot be minimized. In nine cases out of ten the foundations are laid at the primary and secondary schools. The psychologists would of course trace it to the mother's lap, the influence of which is undeniably deep and abiding.

Nevertheless, it is at the higher educational level that the formation of the intellectual begins to take shape. It is there that he is exposed to the vast and complex world of knowledge which has been preserved through centuries in colleges and universities and other research centres. The primary and school education only prepares him for this unique occasion of his initiation into the heritage of knowledge. Whether the rich heritage inspires him to further contribute or just live with it will depend to a certain degree upon his schooling, though fortunately, this is not always true. Some minds, the more sensitive ones, get bored with the cold formalism of school education and burgeon forth vigorously in the relatively freer climate prevailing at the institutions of higher learning.

At this stage it would be helpful to clarify the terms: the literate, the educated and the intellectual. The literate is the one who has learnt to decipher the alphabet, sometimes words and sentences, though with some difficulty. This is the minimum; at the maximum level, he is able to read and write in his own language, sometimes in a foreign language too, though he cannot understand literary language, his own or foreign. Nor can he get at the meaning of a passage dealing with an abstract subject-matter, even though he might be able to read it well.

The educated is distinguished from the mere literate by his acquaintance with the subjects of his study, and by his ability to express his knowledge and understanding with a fair amount of clarity in his own or a foreign language. Apart from his being conversant with the subjects of his study, he is also expected to be aware of the general history of mankind, his own civilization and culture in comparison and contrast to others. He has cultivated in addition, a sense of self-discipline, that is, learnt to exercise restraint in the expression of his emotions and in his behaviour in dealing with others. He is generally dutiful and law-abiding in all spheres of his life.

The intellectual however, is an adventure in the world of ideas and thought. He is a much freer spirit than the educated could ever be in practice, though the latter might sometimes dream of it. The intellectual begins where the educated stops. The educated gathers unto his mind some part of the existing knowledge, the intellectual tries to comprehend the entire stock of existing knowledge in his specialized field, and then to contribute to it himself. The intellectual extends the frontiers of knowledge; his greatness is related to the nature and value of this extension. He is both the consumer of existing ideas, and the producer of new ones.

The distinction between the educated and the intellectual is not very sharp. A well-educated person has all the potentiality of the intellectual; but whether he does become one depends upon his *will-power* which, in turn, depends upon the kind of nerves he has inherited and the social-cultural environment in which he lives.

Now it might be said that while the job of schools is to make children literate, that of colleges is to make them educated. The job of universities on the one hand is to continue the process of education at a higher level and, on the other, to provide at the same time, an atmosphere of free intellectual inquiry.

Unfortunately in India, the process of literacy continues through schools to colleges, and often to universities as well. The best colleges and the best universities at the best of their times have produced m rely the well-educated, with the least inclination for intellectual adventure, and also the least capacity for it. It is when some of the best ones chance to go to western universities that they become aware of the existence of the intellectual world; and only a negligibly few of them get infected with the curiosity for exploring the mysteries of this world. No wonder that all distinguished Indian intellectuals have been and are even now trained for intellectual life at western universities.

In a sense this should not be surprising. Good and great universities take centuries to build up their character; whereas the oldest of the Indian universities at Calcutta, Bombay and Madras are not even a century and a half old.

Nevertheless, this is a sufficiently long period of time for a university to develop, or at least, to begin to develop its own traditions and conventions of higher research. Lamentably, nothing of this kind is anywhere in sight. In comparison some of the universities established later have fared much better, though they would stand nowhere in comparison to the world's famous universities. In the building up of a university, isolated successes and eminences do not count for much. The growth of a free intellectual life, of a distinct school of thought and tradition of research, are infinitely more important.

There are clearly reasons why Indian universities have not been able to achieve anything of this kind. First, they were established by the foreign colonial power and did not grow out of the native aspirations of the people. Their courses of study were framed specifically for the purpose of producing educated men for government jobs, loyal to the British regime in India. Secondly, the Indian people in general did not take to university education quickly. They frankly disapproved of it and would not allow their children to receive it, except in big cities where the cultural resistance to English education had already weakened by the contact with the British people. Thus the universities functioned almost in complete isolation from the real lives of the people, a tiny fraction of whom chose to come up to the university level of education.

These two reasons make it also clear that the whole and

sole objective set before the three earliest universities, as also of all those established later, was just to *educate* the people, not to provide facilities for the growth of the intellectual. In fact, some of the universities established later were required to conduct high-school examinations and distribute matriculation certificates, which thus tended to reduce the job of the university to the promotion of mere literacy as well.

In view of the situation prevailing at that time and continuing basically unaltered till independence, it is understandable why the universities were not induced to perform the functions appropriate to them, that is, to disseminate existing knowledge and produce more. The rulers were interested only in creating hands for the clerical jobs to run the empire, and the people were interested only in keeping to their traditional ways. For both literacy in the new medium of English was of utmost importance. It opened up a vast treasure house of world knowledge, and the more inquisitive minds could go ahead after they had become literate and acquired at least the rudiments of modern education. These minds then could travel to the really great modern universities in Britain and other European countries.

That the same situation should have been allowed to continue even after independence is not understandable. In this respect it was not the same situation as before; it became much worse. Before independence closer links existed between the Indian universities and the British universities. Frequent visits of British and European scholars to the Indian universities made the transmission of knowledge quick and easy. Indian scholars too were induced and helped to visit universities abroad and profit immensely by studies there. What helped the growth of university education in India during those days was that the universities were kept free from political activities, though, fortunately, not from political education as such. In keeping with their tradition at home the British rulers in India did not interfere with the universities in their curricular or extra-curricular affairs. A fairly conducive atmosphere prevailed on the campuses, for the dissemination and growth of knowledge.

After independence the links with the British universities naturally weakened and became uncertain, following a confusion of educational objectives in India. With the assertion of narrow chauvinistic sentiments the blame for all ills in the Indian society was laid on the British rule and English education. For a few years the British universities were regarded commonly as breeding ground of only sahibs. Soon with the retaining of the English medium of instruction at the college and university level and Jawaharlal Nehru's endeavour to initiate the process of modernization on the British pattern, the prestige of the British universities revived. Because the process of modernization remained limited to the superficial aspects of society, Indian scholars started coming to British universities not in pursuit of knowledge but of degrees, which assured their social and economic status at home. This was encouraged by a totally anglicized bureaucracy as well. As a result of this the Indian universities continued to be treated both by government and people as institutions merely disseminating primary knowledge, not of creating it.

The situation became much worse in another sense. The universities in free India turned into a hot-bed of cheap political activities indulged in both by students and teachers. Of course, the process of politicizing the university community had begun with the advent of Gandhi on the Indian political scene. Using the student and teacher power, which had grown to considerable strength by the twenties, for political purposes was one of the main planks of the Gandhian program of action. It was then that the general disaffection towards modern knowledge had been bred. These tendencies naturally grew to most alarming proportions only after a few years of attaining independence. Academic issues came to be constantly subordinated to political issues, often petty and frivolous in nature.

There is no doubt that Jawaharlal Nehru was a great advocate of the necessity of acquiring and ultimately creating modern knowledge. He often dreamt of India one day becoming the pioneer of modern knowledge in various disciplines. In pursuit of his dream he promoted the growth of the existing universities and established new ones of specialized nature. Soon a number of engineering and agricultural universities came into being, with adequate financial grants for conducting research and training. Through the acts of Parliament a number of more privileged and more affluent universities were initiated, called the central universities, of which Delhi University was intended to become a model institution. In addition also were established a number of schools, institutes, councils, national laboratories, wholly concerned with higher research in both natural and social sciences. On the cultural front, the Akademies were established to restore to an order India's rich cultural heritage, to reinterpret it in modern terms and thereby show its relevance to the making of modern Indian society. Thus the Akademies too were meant to be research centres, in addition to extending patronage to literature and the arts.

Most of these centres of higher learning and higher original research, backed by ample financial provision and housed in ultra-modern buildings with all conveniences, started functioning between the years 1950 and 1954. By 1964 these much applauded, much publicized centres already started showing signs of decaying into being no more than extensions of government administrative departments. They came to be concerned more with file-work, that is formal work done as a matter of duty, than with the higher research work which had been entrusted to them. Intenecine rivalry, clamour for promotion to higher grades, squabble for petty gains became rampant. By 1974 it was clear beyond doubt that they would never be able to deliver goods of any worth.

As for college and university education, the situation is much more baffling. There has been an extraordinary increase in the number of colleges and universities all over India, and more in the number of students coming up to these institutions. Colleges have sprouted in villages, and universities in suburban towns. The number of teachers employed in colleges and universities would alone probably amount to a million or so.

Yet what is the achievement of these institutions, in terms of higher education and research? Practically nil. If they have served or are serving any purpose, it is primarily that of disseminating literacy and only occasionally knowledge, the purposes which should more appropriately have been served by primary and secondary schools.

One of the most important reasons why Indian universities have not been able to build up their own distinct character is the constant and almost total government control over them since their inception. In pre-independence days it was the control of the colonial government; afterwards, it was the national government. Both have used them to serve their own ends, with a difference, however. While the ends of the colonial government were clear and, to howsoever limited an extent, conducive to the growth of higher knowledge, the ends of the national government are confused with an utter lack of direction.

The government control is inevitable and unavoidable when the universities and centres of research in India have always been founded with entire monetary support from its coffers. Not a single university in India has been established with funds from private endowments, except the Pilani University of Engineering and Technology by the Birlas. The reason why this has been so is pretty clear. The masses in India never felt the urge for acquiring modern education; they do not feel it even today. They still do not find it relevant to their social and cultural life. They would certainly engage themselves in research, but only so far as that was required to fetch them the degree of Ph.D. necessary for promotion in the servrce. This explains the plethora of Ph.D. theses prepared at the Indian universities, but the almost total lack of a book of original ideas or results in original scientific research.

It has always been the job of the government in India, foreign or national, to provide modern education and initiate steps for modernizing the society. In these circumstances government control becomes unavoidable. However this should not impede the growth of the universities, if government policy is clear about the objective of education, which in turn is vitally dependent upon the objectives and direction of the government's national, political and social policies.

Whatever the objectives, government control on the universities anywhere is bound to restrict intellectual freedom, without which no university can perform its legitimate function. Since the government is run by a handful of alienated intellectuals who subdue the masses by propagating cheap nationalistic sentiments, it leads to the crippling of the proper functioning of the universities. The government cannot dispense with the universities; on the contrary, it must build up more of them at least in respect to structural appearance and paraphernalia. Yet government control tends to affect deleteriously the essential functioning of the universities, in respect to framing the courses of study particularly the social sciences, curricular and extra-curricular activities and the building up of an intellectual community. This is as much true of the universities in India as of those in other Afro-Asian countries.

In India the problem is much more complex. Here the tension between the academic demands of the universities and the political needs of the government is more fundamental and acute. In the Afro-Asian world, India perhaps is the only country where cultural traditions of philosophy, literature, the arts and the folk-lores are still fully alive in the beliefs, attitudes and conduct of the people. These vital religious-cultural traditions of India have withstood the rise of Buddhism, the onslaught and appeasement of the Muslim rulers and, finally, the modernizing impact of the British rulers. These traditions absorb new influences and mould tnem completely into their own beliefs and practices. Far from changing under the impact of modern education and modern science, the Indian cultural traditions have used them to fortify their own anti-intellectual outlook and beliefs.

Modern knowledge is cited in support of the eternal validity of the unchanging Indian tradition. This involves more than a travesty of logic; it involves a strong and deep sense of refusal to recognize the validity of the intellect to comprehend and explain life and the universe. This explains the phenomenal growth of Indian yogis and rishis in the twentieth century who use jetplanes and electronic gadgets to teach meditation and Krishna consciousness and what-not. They are, of course, the cleverer traditionalists ready to exploit the gullible in the west; but they also embody the predominent anti-intellectual traits of Indian cultural tradition.

In universities in India, because of the stringent hold of these anti-intellectual and religious-traditions on the teachers and students, a tension is simultaneously generated on two levels: cultural and political. On both levels, the tension impedes the growth of free inquiry and thereby the acquisition as well as production of knowledge.

On the cultural level, the tension arises out of the conflict between the demand of the intellect to inquire into the nature of things, and the lack of will to pursue the inquiry. As college and university teachers grow older, their intellectual curiosity, even if they had any, grows cool and soon completely disappears. The inner deep-seated anti-intellectual cultural faith asserts itself to make them view all intellectual work as no more than utilitarian, and turn to some kind of spiritualism for salvation. Eminent professors of even such modern subjects as physics, political science, economics, English literature and history have turned to spiritualism and yoga. They publicly offer from the university platform justifications for spiritualism and denounce the pursuit of modern knowledge as delusion. The impact of all this on the students can only be imagined. With whatever readiness they join the universities, it evaporates as they come into contact with their teachers.

On the political level, the tension "arises from," to use Edward Shils's words, "nationalistic sensitivity of the latter (that is, the political world) to the inherent cosmopolitanism of the intellectual community."[1] Freedom to the Afro-Asian countries, including India, came not as a result of espousing the cause of modernity but of arousing the sentiments of national pride which in India meant pride in the glorious past. But ironically enough, the political elite which aroused these sentiments was itself the product of modern education. So the political-intellectual leaders would regulate the sentiments of the masses to an extent and in a manner that serve their own political purpose fairly well. But whatever the extent and the manner, the national traditions and achievements of the past would not legitimately find a place in the curricula of a modern university which are wholly based on the knowledge generated and accumulated, and still being generated and accumulated in the West. Thus the teaching of modern knowledge does not contribute anything to the inflation of sentiments of national glorification, which the government leaders find irksome. And therefore, they try to force the universities to dilute modern knowledge in a manner that it justifies national pride. The universities have thus to come lose their legitimate and proper character and become tools in the hands of politicians.

If the two levels of tension are viewed simultaneously as they should be, it should not surprise us why an atmosphere of

---

[1] E. Shils, *Modernization and Higher Education.*

total stagnation prevails in the Indian universities, including those model ones which were established with so much of fanfare. Not that no work is being done, but not the kind of work modern universities are expected to do. Most work is repetition and imitation of what has already been done in the western world. No pioneering work is being done anywhere. What is more lamentable, absolutely no attempt at doing pioneering work is made at any university. It seems to be a tacitly accepted assumption of both the government, whatever its leaders might profess, and the universities, that original research work is just not possible in this country. Therefore, they would not care for spending adequate sums on providing adequate research facilities, libraries, and, above all, incentives to higher research. When there is a cut in the central and state budgets, the universities have to bear the major brunt of it. In a country which needs modern education to foster its own sound intellectual traditions, the universities should have been given top-priority, for they remain the most important means of modernizing and democratizing a society. But as things have come to pass, they are given the lowest priorities, with the result that only a facade of modern education is kept up, behind which is nothing but monotony and routine-work. Naturally the more inquisitive minds have tried to migrate to the universities of the west, and out of them quite a few, working in more conducive circumstances, contributed significantly to the world knowledge, notable amongst those being Hargovind Khorana and Narlikar.

It sounds ridiculous when the Indian government with crocodile tears in its eyes laments over brain-drain, and appeals to Indian personalities abroad to return home in the name of patriotism. It is natural that the appeal should fail, for patriotism is not sufficiently strong a sentiment to bring them back. The seekers of higher knowledge belong to a larger community than patriotism can comprehend, and are lured to places which promise them adequate facilities and full freedom in their intellectual work. The day these will be available, the Indian brains will begin to return home without any appeal whatsoever.

At present however, the stagnation at the heart of the university life continues, though it is being covered up by a spurt of pseudo-intellectual activities, some of which, in absence of real intellectual achievements, are vociferously acclaimed in a poor bid to justify the existence of the university life. In consequence a confusion of values has come to prevail in the Indian universities. Textbooks are taken for original works, and Sunday magazine articles are hailed as contribution to knowledge, depending of course, upon who is the writer and who is the assessor. And when superficiality passes for genuine stuff, academic intrigues and political manoeuvrings are bound to become the order of the day. But the order is otherwise in the case of the Indian universities. It is because of the rise of academic intrigues and introduction of political manoeuvrings in the universities that the superficiality began to pass for genuine stuff.

The essay referred to above by Edward Shils, after discussing the causes of decay in the universities of the third world, suggests that all steps must be taken "to fortify the intellectual will of the university teachers. This fortification is not, however, just a matter of institutional arrangement.... It also calls for the strength of character on the part of the university staff members..."

In India unfortunately, after Nehru, more steps have been taken rather to weaken "the intellectual will" (presuming it was there in the teachers) and "strength of character." And the compulsions have not always been political; more insistent have been the cultural compulsions.

Chapter Eleven

AN ELITE WITHOUT IDENTITY:DELHI INTELLECTUALS X-RAYED

With individual and ideological variations, the intellectual elites of almost every metropolis in the world have acquired an identity of their own. London intellectuals, however sharply they may differ from, or even oppose each other in their approaches to problems, have something distinctive which derives from their being Londoners. One could not, for example, place Bertrand Russell in New York, nor, for that matter, Professor Galbraith in London. Nor could Malcolm Muggeridge, with all his journalistic flair, ever be associated with Washington. Finally, no other metropolis but Paris could have given the particular flavour that one finds in Sartre or Mauriac or Malraux.

While the original ideas produced by intellectuals anywhere in the world certainly gain wide acceptance, the intellectuals themselves are to an extent the product of the metropolitan milieu from which they hail. They are as much moulded by the general intellectual climate of the metropolis they have grown in as they, in turn, mould the life of their metropolis.

Thus every metropolis in the intellectual world comes to acquire in course of time an identity which lends, in turn, an identity to its intellectuals too. This identity is not easy to define, but it is unmistakably reflected in the tone and temper and the total life-view of the intellectuals. A Marxist intellectual of London, for instance, is not the same as another Marxist intellectual of Paris or, say, of Tokyo. The living cultural and intellectual traditions of a metropolis, the kind of climate prevailing at its institutions, the pattern of education given at its schools and colleges and universities, its economic and social systems, in fact, the whole complex history behind a metropolis, determines the nature of its identity as also of its intellectuals.

Of the four metropolitan cities within India, Calcutta, Bombay, and Madras can with some justification lay claims to having intellectual traditions, and hence distinct identities of their own. Of the late nineteenth century cultural renaissance in India, Calcutta-based intellectuals were, as we all know, the great pioneers. Very often since then, the most avant-garde cultural and intellectual movements have been emanating mostly from Calcutta. Even today, when there are admittedly clear signs of decline in Calcutta's intellectual-cultural life, its intellectuals have a distinct force about them, a raciness which is characteristically their own, and which derives from the long and rich nationalist tradition of the metropolis.

Similarly Bombay intellectuals carry about them their suavity, calculatedness and composure which also characterises their approach to intellectual problems.

As for Madras, the intellectuals there have mostly come from the Brahmin caste and have excelled in philosophy, mathematics and the natural sciences. They have grown up in the sanskritic tradition and are characterised by a pundit-like approach to problems of the contemporary world. Rooted in the sanskrit culture, the Madras intellectuals tend to absorb modernity without becoming modern in their everyday life or family or social dealings. They are distinguished by a sharpness of perception in abstract problems, mathematical as well as spiritual.

As compared to the other three Indian metropolises, Delhi is a city of anomalies, anachronisms and queer contradictions. Delhi has a chequered history behind it, glimmering with variegated colours of myths and legends, fancies and facts, and the reigns of emperors great and small. For the same reason perhaps, Delhi has not been able to acquire an individuality of its own in the intellectual realm. Consequently today, despite the fact that history has enjoined on it to play the role of an intellectual metropolis, it is one without any discernibly distinctive identity. A lack of this identity explains to some extent some of the characteristic traits of the Delhi intellectual elites.

In the recorded chronicle of Delhi, the Moghul emperors were the first who tried to turn the city into a metropolis reflecting the splendours of their time. Before that Delhi was a city of amorphous and uncertain character. The great Moghuls imprinted their own stamp on it, so that before the advent of the British Raj, Delhi was apparently, and for all purposes, turned into a Moghul city. The ancient elements, the mythical and the legendary, were submerged under the flood of Moghul splendour. Then came the Britishers from Calcutta, Bombay and Madras. For quite many years after the establishment of the Raj, Delhi's intellectuals, if the term could be applied to them, were the debilitated erstwhile courtiers of the Moghul empire. They consisted of sycophants, parasites, pretenders. After the total seizure of Delhi in 1857, these courtier-intellectuals found themselves bereft of any support or succour, deprived of the subject matter, the very goal of their "intellectual" deliberations. The white-skinned lords of the New Raj did not need them, at least for the purpose they had "intellectually" trained themselves. Later on some English-educated intellectuals of the next generation adjusted themselves to the new circumstances without much discomfort, but most of them still felt orphaned.

With the shifting of the capital of British India from Calcutta to Delhi in 1912, Delhi once again became the seat of political and administrative power. This was not true of intellectual activities, of which Calcutta, Bombay and Madras continued to be the centres. Some provincial cities too such as Patna, Allahabad, Lucknow, Nagpur, Poona, Mysore, had more than a proportionate share of intellectual activities in comparison to Delhi. At that time Delhi's intellectuals invariably consisted of Britishers, the administrators, the bureaucrats, the jurists and the journalists and writers visiting India. It was a closed circle to which the native "intellectuals," if any, had no access. This was not so much on account of the colour bar. To members of the British intellectual circle, the native "intellectuals" were almost wholly incomprehensible. Language of course was a barrier, but more formidable was the huge gap of some centuries between the two groups in respect to mental attitudes, the quality of education and the general outlook on life.

As the struggle for national independence caught on, intellectuals from all parts of the country, now English-educated and acquainted, started migrating to Delhi, some for temporary visits, some to settle down. These were of two categories, those who came as supporters and servants of the ruling clan, such as Indian ICS, IPS, IES men and other departments of the government; and secondly, those who were champions of self-rule and wished to stay tactically close to the seat of power. Between these two groups, both consisting of outsiders, there was always some tension caused by their mutually opposed objectives. The "free" intellectuals were insignificant in number, much less educated and skilful and much less trained for intellectual activities than the "official" intellectuals.

Ever since the disintegration of Moghul rule and establishment of the British Raj, Delhi's own contribution to the number or quality of intellectuals in the city has always been negligible. During Moghul days, *madrasas* were thought to provide the ideal education. Urdu was the language of the educated, and the education given was almost wholly religious in character with some mathematics, history and geography. As for the few Hindus in Delhi, the orthodox ones withdrew further into their Sanskrit texts while others, driven by the necessity of work, took to Urdu education for this purpose.

With the advent of the British Raj and contact with the west, the Urdu-medium education was relegated to the same level of importance as Sanskrit and Hindi. Now education came to mean the English-medium, comprising of the English language and subjects such as modern mathematics, economics, civics, history, physical and political geography, philosophy, and the natural sciences. After an initial period of hesitation, both Muslims and Hindus, excepting the few staunchly religious ones, happily started joining the English medium schools and later colleges. This was the beginning of modern education in Delhi, though curiously as late as the nineteen twenties this education was available only through the school level.

Delhi did not have its own university until 1921. In north India Calcutta University in the eastern wing and Punjab University in the western wing enjoyed great eminence. Delhi had only three colleges then, which were affiliated to the Punjab University. Thus the beginning of modern education in Delhi could be traced to the establishment of Delhi University in 1922. By then the Calcutta, Bombay and Madras Universities were about sixty five years old. Even after its establishment, for many years, Delhi University remained only an examining University, acting almost as a subsidiary of the Punjab University, and never showed any inclination of becoming a seat of learning.

With the attainment of independence, the picture changed radically. With the government policy to provide modern education to the largest possible number of people, there occurred a phenomenal increase in the number of colleges and the university teaching departments. This was particularly so after it was made, along with four other universities, a central university by an Act of the Parliament in 1952. Today, Delhi University has over sixty colleges and institutes affiliated to it, apart from its own departments of post-graduate teaching.

In addition there is the highly prestigious Jawaharlal Nehru University with the avowed objective of conducting high level research in social sciences and the languages. This was established in 1967-1968, with the hopes that it would become a fountain of original ideas. Best minds in the various disciplines available in the country and on the best of the terms were enlisted to work at the JNU and produce intellectual matter of top class.

Apart from these two distinguished universities, Delhi has the fortune of having some social sciences research institutes of government and semi-government, not to mention the numerous private research organisations.

Thus, whatever the lack of opportunities for intellectual work during the pre-independence days, today they abound in Delhi. Ever since independence, it has been the tacit but determined endeavour of the national government to turn Delhi, the seat of ultimate political power, into the seat of the ultimate intellectual power. It was with this objective in view that so many schools and councils were founded in Delhi: the Delhi School of Economics, Delhi School of Social Work, School for International Studies, Indian Council for Social Science Research and so on and so forth. All these high-grade schools and institutes and councils, whether within or without the jurisidiction of the two universities, are richly financed and are well equipped with the tools of research, even in accordance with the prevailing international standards.

Yet keeping in view the international standard of intellectual attainment, or even the national standard, has Delhi created for itself an intellectual standard? The only and the unequivocal answer is "No."

What has gone wrong?

First, despite the proliferation of research institutes and organisations in Delhi since independence, Delhi has produced no intellectual of its own, even of mediocre order. None of the intellectuals of any merit today was born and bred in Delhi. All of them have come from outside the capital and have remained outsiders, tending to owe allegiance more to the regions they have come from them, to the city they live in, or the institutions they work with. They are not inclined to build up a Delhi School of Thought, or evolve a system of original ideas relevant to the national as well as international problems. This demands an involvement in intellectual work which can come only from having a sense of national, as distinguished from regional identity, as well as well-defined social, political and economic objectives.

Quite aside from the fact that the conditions urging intellectuals to be involved in their work have been lacking, other factors have also largely contributed to the diffusion and waste of intellectual energy in Delhi.

First, the intellectuals who migrate to Delhi from other regions of the country do not consider the city as their goal. To them Delhi is a stepping stone to visits abroad, not one or two visits, but several. The rule is : the greater the intellectual, the more frequent his visit to foreign countries. In fact, the number of visits he makes to foreign countries is often considered to determine his stature and authority in his field. This happens because intellectuals having come to Delhi soon realise that Delhi is a city without any roots of its own. In the world of intellectuals, far from being a metropolis, it is merely a provincial town. A desire to visit the world intellectual metropolises is understandable. Yet through a peculiar alchemy of the Indian character, this desire is not born of a genuine urge to equip one's intellectual powers more richly and train oneself in free intellectual thinking. The visit abroad becomes a status symbol and position of authority which subdues the indigenous intellectuals into submission. These intellectuals too in turn wait for their opportunities to visit abroad, and sometimes the unfortunate ones wait all their lives.

Secondly, there is the attraction of the Central Government offices in such capacities as consultants and advisors which carry immense authority, power and privilege. This is possible only when intellectuals live in Delhi, close to the corridors of political power, and keep hobnobbing with rulers of various levels. This proximity tempts the intellectuals to migrate to Delhi, but not to develop as free thinkers. They come to exploit the immense possibilities inherent in proximity to governmental power. Once they procure admissions for themselves to the government offices and jobs, they cease to be free intellectuals, and lose their identity altogether.

Thus, intellectuals who come to Delhi do so either with a view primarily to making trips abroad, or procuring government assignments, or both, since one can and often does lead to the other. As for the local intellectuals, there are at present perhaps none. While a typical Calcuttan, a typical Bombayite, a typical Madrasi may have some intellectual pretensions, a typical Delhiwalla has absolutely none. For one thing, it is difficult to define a Delhiwalla. When Delhi was made Indian's capital, its population was meagre. A great majority of the local population was Muslim, though by then a number of non-Muslim people had migrated from the Punjab in search of trade and business. Until 1947 this population had not increased appreciably, but after 1947 with the refugees from Pakistan, the population started suddenly to grow. Among them there were only a few intellectuals, and the traumatic shock of partition had made them lose all their zest for intellectual work. They sought desperately just to keep themselves alive, either by taking to trade and commerce or taking up whatever jobs the government offered them. They had nothing whatever to do with intellectual pursuits.

In the past thirty years since independence and partition, another generation of fresh minds have grown up in Delhi. They comprise the children of both the traditional Delhiwallas and of the emigrant refugees from Pakistan. They have grown up in relatively better circumstances which should have instilled into them at least an inclination for intellectual curiosities. Yet they seem to have inherited a distrust of intellectual pursuits, which has been further "enriched" by Delhi's traditional culture. They have put all their trust in money-making activities, fair or foul, and in enjoying the pleasures of life. Their modernity is only skin-deep, in fact not even skin-deep. They make no pretence whatsoever to thinking anything for themselves, they take no decisions and they undergo no intellectual or emotional crises. Life is them is easily comprehensible in the same terms as it was to their fathers and grand fathers. Temporarily some of them might strike a revolutionary or a radical pose, but soon they come round to settle down in life almost exactly with the same attitudes to life as their forefathers.

No wonder then, that Delhi is one of the most unintellectual, if not anti-intellectual, capital of the world. The anti-intellectualism of pre-British Moghul days has come to be reinforced with the anti-intellectualism of the post-British and the post-partition culture. Intellectual pursuits are performed by the outsiders, who are fully aware that even for an initial acknowledgement of their intellectual work, they cannot depend upon the Delhiwallas. These pseudo-intellectuals are free to make tall claims to originality and demands for public support, for Delhi's intellectual atmosphere does not sift the pseudo from the genuine.

It is not without significance that Delhi catches quickly all those aspects of modern culture which are anti-intellectual in nature. The cinema, TV, cabaret, wrestling, sports and games, mushairas, stage sex-plays and film-stars nites abound in Delhi, and fetch infinitely larger crowds here than in any other metropolitan city in India. Not even one per cent of these crowds would be seen in any of the several libraries in the city.

During the past thirty years several centres of intellectual discussion and debate have come up with similar intentions as the Delhi Schools of higher studies, but have also lost out in the confusion. Not a single one of them can claim to have helped build up a distinct body of thought and ideas relevant to the life today in India. At best, they have made available to the few Delhi intellectuals, pseudo or real but all outsiders, the thought and ideas produced abroad, particularly in the west. Although that in itself is desirable, the basic objective of letting foreign ideas fertilize the local intellectual mind has remained so far an unrealised dream.

Delhi intellectuals, drawn from different provinces of the country, have remained diehard traditionalists, totally immune to the impact of modern education or the changing modern industrial society. They have created a variety of cultural activities in the city and, in a sense, provide proof of the jargon, "unity in diversity."

A discriminatory look at these cultural activities will reveal that they are basically unintellectual, if not anti-intellectual, activities. They are backward-looking and nostalgic, lulling the mind into soporofic indolence. This is the unifying principle in the diversity of Indian culture. All our classical dance, classical music, classical poetry, in other words, is devoid of thought-content and replete with the subtleties of sex-content.

The increasing insistence on the revival of folk culture is part of contemporary India's anti-intellectual drive. This works nowhere else with so much success as in Delhi, where the general intellectual level of even the educated class has remained at the folk level. This explains the growth of *Hanuman* temples and other places of worship in Delhi, and the small and big conferences of different religions in the city. Leaders of all religions, without exception, desperately seek the protection and the patronage of the central government. The religious leaders find the place convenient for another reason, since here they will never fall short of an audience. There is always a ready audience for every function, from *Bhagwati Jagran* in a mohalla street to bicentennial celebrations of different religious orders in the Ramlila Maidan. A greater portion of the crowds which assemble at several Hanuman temples on Tuesdays also consist of Delhi intellectuals, high government officials, members of legislative bodies, science, teachers, journalists, business executives, writers, lawyers, doctors, engineers, not to mention the seasonal rush of college boys seeking the blessings of the gods and goddesses during exams, and of college girls for marriage.

In such a tribal atmosphere which prevails under the tinsel, is it possible for an intellectual to emerge, and then maintain the tempo of his intellectual activities? An intellectual does not grow in isolation. He owes his existence to the general intellectual milieu prevailing around him, from which he derives his character, strength and vision, and to the enrichment of which all his intellectual activities are directed.

Chapter Twelve

RESPONSIBILITIES OF THE INDIAN INTELLECTUAL

The responsibilities of the Indian intellectual emanates from the nature of his emergence as a social and political force during the hey-day of the British regime, from the nature of his fight for freedom and finally, from the nature of the freedom itself which was attained for the country.

The intellectuals emerged as a social and political force only after they had received English liberal-scientific education, imbibed European thought and personally observed the working of British society. Before this, the Indian intellectuals had flourished in isolation from the social-political context. They attained spiritual, artistic, and literacy excellences individually, the impact of which remained limited to the fragments of communities to which they belonged. During the British rule they rose above their communities, and began to speak for the larger Indian society in a language that was understood from one end of the now vast country to the other.

When they rose as a group demanding a share in colonial administration and, later, demanding complete political freedom, they assumed a role which properly speaking the intellectuals are not expected to play. The job of the intellectuals is to devote themselves to the pursuit of knowledge and abstain themselves from political intrigues and squabbles. The course of contemporary history however, inspired the Indian intellectuals to assume the role of social and political leaders, which they did with great enthusiasm.

Here the distinction from the European or, for that matter, American intellectuals, is sharp indeed. These western intellectuals did not have to fight for political freedom. Of course they had to fight for intellectual freedom, but this was a fight which was unavoidably related to their very functioning as intellectuals. They never fought for assuming the responsibilities of social and political leadership and governing their countries. They certainly produced ideas, powerful and compelling ideas which toppled empires and roused people to violent revolutions, but they never participated in the battle to acquire political power. They fought as intellectuals and, whatever the consequence of the battle, emerged as intellectuals, preoccupied with their intellectual work. Galileo, Kepler, Milton, Luther, Dryden, Rousseau, Marx, Darwin, Flaubert, Dostoevsky, Tolstoy, Gorki, Einstein and Sartre are among hundreds of others who illustrate this point at issue.

The Indian intellectuals, however, were destined to act the role which was not appropriate to their education or training or experience. Yet they played the role amazingly well and effectively, and not for political freedom alone. In fact, it was impossible for them to forget that they were primarily intellectual and not a pack of power-hungry politicians. That is why they never got tired of reiterating that political freedom was not the end; it was only a means to attaining and enjoying full intellectual freedom.

Naturally therefore, when freedom came, the first thing the intellectual-politicians ensured was full intellectual freedom which is always congruent with individual liberty. They not only enshrined it in clear terms in the Constitution of Free India. In fact, the entire Constitution, every clause of it, was imbued with the spirit of guaranteeing, protecting and enriching intellectual freedom.

Soon, however, the inherent contradictions in the intellectuals being the rulers arose. With rulers inevitably comes power and authority, and with power and authority comes political manipulation and intrigue. To have obtained power from the foreign ruler was one thing, but to remain in power as the political support become another matter. They had to rule as administrators suddenly facing the baffling complexities of the social, political and cultural realities, which required to be tackled with more of commonsense and tact than with abstract intellectual ideas.

Nevertheless, the intellectual-politicians who obtained freedom and were trained in the course of struggle for both constitutional and administrative work, faced the odds boldly and imaginatively. In dealing with the foreign rulers, the intellectual-politicians were dealing with their equals whose language and behaviour they fully understood. In dealing with the masses now they had to tackle the illiterate, the ignorant, the superstitious, with the least idea of what political freedom meant. let alone intellectual freedom. The temptation to rule over them tyrannically, to teach them things of modern civilization and modern culture with the help of the rod, was great. But the intellectual-political leaders, now turned rulers, chose the more daring way of teaching the masses their own responsibility: through involving them, howsoever imperfectly in the beginning, in the open democratic process of nation-building. The progress was bound to be slow and halting, sometimes greatly irritating to the intellectual nation-builders. A few of them even expressed their preference for a dictatorial type of government, for the speedy implementation of the economic plans. The leaders at the helm of national affairs never for a moment, even in theory, succumbed to the idea of undermining the ideals of full intellectual freedom, in the realization of which they had fought for political freedom.

This peculiar historical background defines the responsibilities of the Indian intellectuals today. Having once obtained political freedom from the foreign ruler and become the rulers, they can only at their own peril say that they have nothing to do with politics. In India, fortunately or unfortunately, political awareness was concomitant with intellectual awareness. The intellectuals themselves had to fight for political freedom, and finally they themselves became the political rulers. In their case therefore, intellectual responsibilities can in no case be divorced from political-social responsibilities. They are actually not two kinds of responsibilities, but one.

They must realize that the objectives of full intellectual freedom, to be attained through political freedom, have not yet been realized. In fact, it cannot be realized in a short span of a few decades. It can be realized only after an arduous. persevering and long revolution, continuing through generations The sooner the Indian intellectuals can realize the imperative need of this revolution, the better for them and also for the society in which they live. Since intellectual freedom was the highest ideal for which political freedom was obtained, losing it at any time is bound to lead to the loss of political freedom itself.

In Europe and America the intellectuals do not have to face this dilemma, at least in this acute and perilous form. There the loss of intellectual freedom will certainly lead to totalitarianism and tyranny, but not necessarily to the loss of political freedom. The examples of Nazi Germany, Fascist Italy, Communist Russia exist. In India the situation is different. The country has been free only for thirty years, a relatively short period for a country to become politically, economically and militarily strong and intellectually advanced. In these areas it is still dependent upon the big powers. Once intellectual freedom is lost, it would be easier for one or the other powers to subdue the Indian rulers. For the masses on their own would not still offer any effective resistance to any foreign power, overtly or covertly manipulating to divest the country of its political freedom. To make them fully conscious of the immense value of political freedom and individual liberty is the gigantic task before the Indian intellectuals, as the harbinger and the agent of social and political change.

This change is unmistakably in the direction of the modernization of society in all its aspects. Any wavering from this direction is fraught with the perils of disorder, confusion, chaos. Whether or not the intellectuals in India continue to take the lead in this direction, the process of socio-economic modernization, begun during the Nehru era, must inevitably go on. In absence of the lead which must come from the intellectuals, the process of modernization might lead to only pseudo-modernization, or a half-hearted movement towards modernization. In other words it might lead to the corruption of the process of modernization itself.

The corruption of modernization breeds numerous social evils: bribery, smuggling, black-marketing, tax-evasion and a host of others which infest the Indian society. It breeds educational and cultural evils, such as indolence, impatience, intrigue, search for easy fame and short-cuts to success. It tends, in other words, to create a hollowness in the heart of society. Out of this emerges, surreptitiously but surely, political evils of all kinds, particularly totalitarianism.

In a sense, under a totalitarian regime the pace of social and economic aspects can be considerably accelerated. The Soviet and the Chinese societies provide ample proof of this. Since the people are not involved in the process of taking policy decisions and framing rules of government programs, there is absolutely no procedural delay. The masses take orders and have no option to question or modify them. The same is true of the intellectuals of those societies. The intellectual-politicians having assumed all political power, decide what is good for the people and order the scientists and technologists to devise ways and means of achieving it. The scientific and technological advancement in such circumstances can be amazing, as it is in Russian and Chinese societies. Likewise under Hitler's dictatorship, Germany's achievements in science and technology were astonishingly rapid and fantastic. For a time these achievements added enormously to Germany's economic prosperity and social affluence.

Thus the process of modernization can be quite rapid under a totalitarian regime. Since this is not full nor real modernization, it soon defeats the very purpose and objective behind modernization: to free man from shackles and to enable him to realize his creative potentialities to the full. The real modernization is a total one of man and his society. It is not merely a mechanization of the means of production, or the distribution of wealth on mass scale for mass consumption. It is equally concerned with organizing and evolving such a social and political system which binds man to it, yet leaves him free to realize the way he chooses his intellectual and emotional energies. In the ultimate analysis, modernization is really more deeply concerned with the reorientation of the total outlook of man in society, then with the mere application of science and technology in the production of material wealth. If the process of modernization does not involve the total transformation of man's fundamental attitude to society and the world, and to himself in relation to the other two, it may even lead to a further enslavement of man by other men.

The Indian intellectuals have to see to it that the process of modernization, partially introduced by the British regime and later accelerated by Jawaharlal Nehru, is not deflected from its course or halted half-way. Primarily this is the responsibility of the non-academic intellectuals working in politics, journalism, the legal profession, economic organizations, literature and the fine arts. The academicians too can help substantially by modernizing the syllabuses, and keeping them free from change, and instilling into the young minds the values of modern rational humanism.

Whether the intellectuals will once again, after a decade of prevarication, show readiness to discharge their historical responsibility, will be seen in time. Their readiness must come from strength of will, and that can only come from a fundamental change in the social-cultural attitudes. And there's the rub.

All our great intellectuals in any field belonging to the pre-independence days shared unshakably their common faith, in the total modernization of the Indian society. Gandhi alone, of course, could be said to be anti-modern; but on a deeper consideration of all the issues involved, it may appear that even he was not. In fact, by his social and religious reform, by upholding the dignity of labour and the dignity of man, he could be said to be the first to have introduced modern values to the millenium-old traditional society. Above all, the fact that he chose Jawaharlal Nehru, and not Rajendra Prasad nor Vinoba Bhave as his political heir, shows his implicit faith in modernization.

Nevertheless, the general masses who went by Gandhi's personal life-style and his prayer-meetings, were unable to see beneath the surface. They were crippled in their understanding of Gandhi by traditional culture, which made them follow the Mahatma blindly and worship him almost as an *avatar* rather than comprehend him rationally.

After independence, it was once again the complete hold of this traditional culture on the masses, and on the intellectuals too that baffled Nehru's herculean endeavour to modernize Indian society. They turned him into a hero, a king, a benevolent dictator and what-not. The modern intellectual in Nehru, having to live up to the image the masses created of him, began to weaken and despair, though he never stopped striving for the goal set before himself.

In the way of modernization and the growth of the intellectual activities, India's greatest hurdle has been its basically anti-intellectual traditional culture. Far from modifying itself to modernity, it traditionalizes the modernity itself, thereby frustrating all attempts. It tends in fact to traditionalize the very agents of modernization in India: the modern intellectuals in both political and non-political spheres.

Broadly speaking, it has created two opposite tendencies in the intellectuals, both baneful to the healthy growth of modern democratic life. First, there is a tendency to escape into some kind of isolated spiritual and saintly life, especially with the advancement of or after middle-age. From Aurobindo to Jayprakash Narayan it has been a familiar pattern: good liberal English education up to the highest academic level, a fiery revolutionary youth, followed by sudden disenchantment with all intellectual activities, leading finally to complete withdrawal from social-political world. Such a drift of the erstwhile powerfull intellectuals of the stature of Aurobindo and Jayprakash Narayan mislead many other lesser intellectuals, more prone to the strong traditional pull, to find peace and salvation beyond the bounds of social activities. The life of the masses is thus left to the mercy of those who happen to be in power, and who in the circumstances are easily tempted to acquire absolute power.

It is quite significant that the ordinary masses of the rural area do not so readily retire from social world and become *sanyasis*. Almost till the end of their lives they work in the fields, look after cattle, take care of the family and participate in the social-cultural deliberations and rituals. The sudden shift from one extreme to the other—from vigorous intellectual life to the completely withdrawn *sanyasi* life is typical of some Indian intellectuals, not of the Indian masses. This is amply supported by the inmates of any *ashram*. Almost all of them are or have been intellectuals: college and university teachers, lawyers, judges of the higher courts, economists, journalists, writers and so on. Of the three stages of human life of the *brahmacharya*, *grahastha* and *vanprastha*, as determined by traditional Hindu religion, the pull of *vanprastha* evidently appears to be strongest on the Indian intellectuals.

The second tendency generated by the deep hold of traditional culture is even more baneful. This works in the subtlest manner possible. This tendency makes the intellectual act always as a leader of the masses and never as one of them. The leader, that is *guru*, is the embodiment of all wisdom, whose pronounced word must be accepted as the final. He expects the masses to follow him even if they do not understand him, to come to him for advice on all problems, private or public, medical or educational, gynaecological or eschatological.

It will be readily seen that both the tendencies have one characteristic in common: isolation from the masses. The *sanyasi* withdraws himself completely from the masses. The *guru* places himself on a pedestal much higher than the reach of the masses. In the decades after independence, the *guru* tendency in the Indian intellectuals also proliferated on an amazing scale. Every intellectual worth anything regarded himself as leader *guru* and expected the masses to follow him rather than other leader *gurus*, for he alone knew the panacea to all ills of the society. The *guru* knows the mysteries of certain *mantras* and *tantras* made by greater *gurus* before him. So the Indian intellectual leader had *mantras* memorized from Marx, Lenin, Mao, Che Guevera, Ho Chi Minh, Sartre, Marcuse, not to mention, Gandhi, the *Geeta*, the *Vedas* and a host of numerous others, and chanted them to the masses. Sometimes the masses followed the *gurus* blindly and created nothing but chaos. Sometimes they did not, and the result was the frustration of the *gurus*.

It is any wonder, in the circumstances, that no political party in India, led by intellectuals, has been able to strike roots in the masses?

The Indian intellectuals must realise that no process of healthy modernization can succeed without the full and voluntary involvement of the masses. They must asked the masses not to do things, but to create such social and economic conditions that induce them to do things. They must not impose duties and compulsions on them, but to give them more and more rights which will make them more fully aware of their duties.

Once the masses are on their own, the intellectuals will be relieved of the responsibility of governing them—a responsibility which history in India has thrust upon them. Then they will be free, like European or American intellectuals, to devote themselves wholly to the pursuit and creation of knowledge.

SELECT BIBLIOGRAPHY

Aron, Raymond, *The Opium of the Intellectuals*, Doubleday, New York, 1957.
Azad, Maulana A.K., *India Wins Freedom*, Orient Longmans, New Delhi, 1960.
Chaudhari, N.C., *The Intellectual in India*, Associated Publishing House, New Delhi, 1967.
Collins and Lapierre, *Freedom at Midnight*, Vikas Publishing House, New Delhi, 1976.
D'cruz (S.J.), Edward, *India: The Quest for Nationhood*, Lalvani Publishing House, New Delhi, 1967.
Desai, A.R. (Ed.), *Modernization of Underdeveloped Societies*, Thacker & Co. Ltd., Bombay, 1971.
Doob, Leonard W., *Becoming More Civilized*, New Haven, Yale, 1960.
Ford, Richard B., *Tradition and Change in Four Societies*, Holt, Reinhart and Winston, New York, 1968.
Gabor, Dennis, *The Mature Society*, Secker and Warburg, London, 1972.
Geertz, Clifford, *Old Societies and New States*, The Free Press of Glencoe, London, 1963.
Hoffer, Eric, *The Ordeal of Change*, Harper and Row, New York, 1963.
Mannheim, Karl, *Essays on Sociology of Culture*, Routledge and Kegan Paul, London, 1962.
Martin (Jr.), Briton, *New India, 1885*, Oxford University Press, New Delhi, 1970.
Mead, Margaret, *Continuties in Cultural Evolution*, University Press, Yale, 1964.
Menon, V.P., *Transfer of Power in India*, Orient Longmans, New Delhi, 1957.
Metcalf, T.R., *Modern India*, Macmillan Company, London, 1971.
Nayer, Baldev Raj, *Modernization Imperative and Indian Planning*, Vikas Publishing House, New Delhi, 1972.
Nettle and Robertson, *International Systems and the Modernization of Societies*, Basic Books, New York, 1968.
Rieff, Philip (Ed.), *On Intellectuals*, Anchor Books, New York, 1970.
Segal Ronald, *The Crisis in India*, Penguin Books, 1965.
Shils, Edward, *The Intellectuals and the Powers*, University of Chicago, 1972.
————,*Centre and Periphery*, University of Chicago Press, Chicago, 1975.
————,*The Intellectual between Tradition and Modernity*, Mouton & Co., The Hague, 1961.

Singer, Milton, *When a Great Tradition Modernizes*, Vikas Publishing House, New Delhi, 1972.

Srinivas, M.N., *Social Change in India*, Los Angeles, California, 1966.

Sovani and Dandekar (Ed.), *Changing India: Essays in Honour of Professor Gadgil* Asia Publishing House, Bombay, 1961.

Toynbee, A.J., *A Study of History*, Oxford University Press, London, 1948.

Weiner, Myron (Ed.), *Modernization: The Dynamics of Growth*, Basic Books, New York, 1966.

————,India: Two Political Cultures," an article included in *Political Culture and Political Development*, Princeton University Press, Princeton, 1969.